FULL
FRONTAL
FASHION

FULL FRONTAL FASHION

NEVER WORRY AGAIN ABOUT WHAT TO WEAR

BY THE CREATORS OF

FULL FRONTAL FASHION TOP TEN

AND MELISSA SONES

℗

A PLUME BOOK

P L U M E
Published by Penguin Group
Penguin Group (USA) Inc., 375 Hudson Street, New York, New York 10014, U.S.A.
Penguin Group (Canada), 10 Alcorn Avenue, Toronto, Ontario, Canada M4V 3B2
(a division of Pearson Penguin Canada Inc.)
Penguin Books Ltd., 80 Strand, London WC2R 0RL, England
Penguin Ireland, 25 St. Stephen's Green, Dublin 2, Ireland (a division of Penguin Books Ltd.)
Penguin Group (Australia), 250 Camberwell Road, Camberwell, Victoria 3124, Australia
(a division of Pearson Australia Group Pty. Ltd.)
Penguin Books India Pvt. Ltd., 11 Community Centre, Panchsheel Park, New Delhi – 110 017, India
Penguin Books (NZ), cnr Airborne and Rosedale Roads, Albany, Auckland 1310, New Zealand
(a division of Pearson New Zealand Ltd.)
Penguin Books (South Africa) (Pty.) Ltd., 24 Sturdee Avenue, Rosebank, Johannesburg 2196, South Africa

Penguin Books Ltd., Registered Offices: 80 Strand, London WC2R 0RL, England

First published by Plume, a member of Penguin Group (USA) Inc.

First Printing, July 2005
10 9 8 7 6 5 4 3 2

CIP data is available.
ISBN 0-452-28666-2

PRINTED IN THE UNITED STATES OF AMERICA
Set in Amasis Light
Designed by Richard Oriolo

ACKNOWLEDGMENTS

Most of you know of Full Frontal Fashion from the weekly television series *Full Frontal Fashion Top Ten* on WE: Women's Entertainment. Now in its fourth season, the series offers fashion and style tips for everyday situations from some of the most creative and connected style-meisters to be found anywhere. It's their insights and the trendsetting observations of the Full Frontal Fashion production team that inspired the publication of this book.

Specifically, we want to thank Heather Lanzetta, Kim Sunshine, John Filimon, Zaida Espada, Katie Davison, Scott Goldberg, and David Kutz of the Full Frontal Fashion team, whose ideas and energy helped make this book happen; Kim Martin, general manager of WE; and Kathleen Farrell, our WE production guru for giving our show a such a gracious home.

Our author, Melissa Sones, is an accomplished fashion journalist and style writer who came to our attention after she penned a story about watching *Full Frontal Fashion* obsessively on cable television. She first became aware of *Full Frontal Fashion*—as did many other New Yorkers—when, five years ago, she found comprehensive coverage of the city's Fashion Week runway shows on the regional Metro television channel. That's where the concept of wall-to-wall fashion coverage began. We were happy to make her part of the Full Frontal Fashion team when the opportunity to produce this book emerged. She tells that the best part of the job was interviewing so many fashionable people for their ideas and insights. Our experience exactly. Among those deserving special thanks are our stylist James Aquiar, our market editor Elaine Francisco, associate market editor Prue Lewington, and photographer Chuck Spang. Finally, for Melissa and for the entire Full Frontal team, we owe our experts many thanks for taking the time to share their hard-earned advice:

Mickey Boardman, deputy editorial director, *Paper*

Lloyd Boston, author and style expert

Suze Yalof Schwartz, executive fashion editor-at-large, *Glamour*

Lucy Sykes-Rellie, editor-at-large, *Marie Claire*

Joan Kaner, senior vice president, fashion director, public relations, Neiman Marcus

Robert Burke, senior vice president and fashion director, Bergdorf Goodman

Avril Graham, executive fashion and beauty editor, *Harper's Bazaar*

Sharon Weil, director of special services, Saks Fifth Avenue

Teri Agins, senior special writer, *The Wall Street Journal*

James Aguiar, celebrity stylist

Rebecca Weinberg, celebrity stylist

Simon Doonan, creative director, Barneys New York

Irenka Jakubiak, editor-in-chief, *Accessories*

Betsey Johnson, designer

Michael Kors, designer

Diane von Furstenberg, designer

Shoshanna Lonstein Gruss, designer

Ippolita, jewelry designer

Evyan Metzner, fashion director, *Self*

Laura Begley, style director, *Travel + Leisure*

Pamela Fiori, editor-in-chief, *Town & Country*

ACKNOWLEDGMENTS

vi

Jesse Garza, creative director and co-owner of Visual Therapy

Jennifer Cattaui, fashion editor

Valerie Steele, director and chief curator of the Museum at the Fashion Institute of Technology

Mandi Norwood, editor-in-chief, *Shop Etc.*

Anne Slowey, fashion news director, *Elle*

Jeffrey Kalinsky, owner, Jeffrey New York and Jeffrey Atlanta

Sasha, hairstylist, Gerard Bollei Salon

Judy Licht, co-host, *Full Frontal Fashion*

Christina Ha, co-host, *Full Frontal Fashion*

Rebecca Budig, host, *Full Frontal Fashion Top Ten*

—GREG MOYER AND ELIZABETH DEWEY
for Full Frontal Fashion

CONTENTS

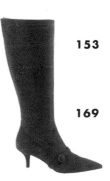

I host *Full Frontal Fashion Top Ten* on We: Women's Entertainment. As the host of such an "on-the-pulse" show as *Full Frontal*, I've realized that I need to keep myself educated on all of the current trends and styles. And in the ever-changing world of fashion, there seem to be few constants.

Growing up in Kentucky in the late 1970s, I felt fashion was more about whatever my sister Shannon wore out on a Saturday night than what graced the covers of any fashion magazines. In fact, my first experience with fashion was wearing Shannon's tubetops and wedge heels as we danced around her bedroom to Elton John's "Honky Cat." Because I have five sisters, each with her own unique sense of style and fashion, I had more influences on a daily basis than most. Perhaps more importantly, we all developed our own unique style so we wouldn't be confused with one another. My sisters and I were also very active in figure skating, gymnastics, dance classes—and all required the appropriate outfits. I was probably more inspired at that time by Dorothy Hamill than Nanette Lepore. Fashion was simply a matter of function for me early on.

Then, from the fourth grade until I graduated from high school, I attended a performing arts school. As I entered my teens, I made the decision to utilize fashion as a way to stand out, to be noticed, and my interest in fashion really began to blossom. I was influenced by the different styles and trends I would see on TV and in the magazines, while trying to add my own personal touch. Once I graduated, I stayed in the midwest for a short time but eventually moved to L.A. to pursue an acting career. As an actress—for auditions, roles, and functions—I would dress appropriately. When I was on my own, though, the fashion choice for me was "comfortable." In fact, it was a running joke that I repeatedly wore the same gray T-shirt over and over again.

As I moved into my twenties and my career became more established, I was exposed to more high-end fashion. It was a new world and it was incredible! When I began my tenure on *All My Children*, I fell in love with Jimmy Choo and Manolo Blahnik. Our stylists on the show have always been interested in making sure we look impeccable, and it rubbed off on me in my personal tastes as well. To that end, fashion became an integral part of my professional and personal life.

I've found that as the host of *Full Frontal Fashion,* I am approached more and more often about fashion. And while I reveal each episode's top ten tips, it occurs to me that I know more about it than I once thought I did. Because of this realization, I have been able to experience a lot of growth in my personal style as well as to become more confident in my clothing selections and tastes. On *Full Frontal Fashion*, we cover each season's latest styles and trends. And as much as I feel I already know about fashion, I learn more useful information with every episode. I hope you find this book just as helpful as you develop your own personal style and pursue the comfortable, the sexy, and the stylish while keeping up with the latest trends in fashion.

—Rebecca Budig for *Full Frontal Fashion Top 10*

FULL
FRONTAL
FASHION

WHAT IS YOUR FASHION PERSONALITY?

Dear Full Frontal Fashion:

As the manager of one of the most popular and fashionable stores in the country, one thing always makes me sad: So many women who shop here simply follow the crowd—everybody wants to do what everybody else does. When I was growing up in the sixties and seventies, things were different. I found a great handmade scarf that nobody else had because I wanted to have my own style; I wore dangling earrings that didn't mimic everyone else's accessories because I knew who I was. Tell me, Full Frontal, what's gone wrong?

SAD IN FASHION LAND

you feel sad, but the truth is that not as much has changed as you may think. After all, most of us want to think of ourselves as rebels with a fashion cause—we want the ability to dress to the nines with creativity and flair. But the fact is, back then, we followed the fashion cycles as slavishly as your customers do today. One thing has really changed, though: There weren't nearly as many choices back then. If you bought a scarf, there was one popular "commercial" look that everyone had and then there was another popular "noncommercial" choice—maybe a one-of-a-kind pick—but very often the look itself was somewhat universal. (Some of us on the Full Frontal Fashion team still own them!)

Back then, too, we all had a wardrobe of "basics." Indeed, fashion experts like us dressed from this (can we say boring?) minimalist list and prescribed the same for everyone else.

Well, welcome to the twenty-first century, where dressing according to your own style—or Fashion Personality—has replaced yesterday's one-size-fits-all approach. Moreover, there has never been a better time to appreciate who you are, fashion-wise. For one thing, there have never been as many designers and fashion companies catering to every "niche" they can find (of course it's "commercial," but it helps you, too), so that finding your Personality or fine-tuning the one you have has never been easier or more exciting.

But the question is—and many of us are in process on this so don't worry—what if you don't know what your Fashion Personality is? As one energetic kindergarten teacher we know lamented, "I had a clairvoyant tell me I hadn't the slightest idea what appearance I wanted to have in this world."

But before we take you on a journey through the Top Ten Fashion Personalities and let you type yourself, we've assembled some preliminary steps for you. Think of these as your Top Ten Stepping Stones to the perfect Fashion Personality for you, highly recommended—and experienced—by all of us on the Full Frontal Fashion style team.

1. **DEVELOP AN EYE.** As style guru Mickey Boardman, the flamboyant deputy editorial director of *Paper*, the cutting-edge magazine, points out, style pros like him often spend ten hours a day in what insiders call "fashion closets"—the dressing rooms the size of small football fields from which editors and stylists select the clothes that models and celebrities wear. Boardman suggests

imitating the pros and visiting as many stores as you can (including ones you wouldn't normally go to) and *trying on as many different styles* as you can. Style expert and author Lloyd Boston also suggests reading fashion magazines and newspapers. Do both, our pros say, until you find the celebrities or style icons whose style you like, then imitate your favorite aspects of it. Finally, *Marie Claire*'s stylish editor-at-large, Lucy Sykes-Rellie, strongly recommends keeping a fashion file or scrapbook of your finds. "Your eye will keep going to the same things and you'll find out what your style is," she says.

2. **LET "IT'S YOU" BE YOUR GUIDE.** While many experts insist there's nothing like a compliment to help you find your fashion self, we say, "Complimentee *beware*." As Sykes-Rellie explains, despite flatterers' good intentions, they're often praising you because you're wearing something unusual—for example, a bright color—and not necessarily because what you're wearing is truly flattering. Moreover, warns Sykes-Rellie, these very flatterers may not exactly have great taste themselves. (*Listen to yourself first* and then, perhaps, to those who tell you that what you're wearing is *"you."*)

3. **LOOK IN THE MIRROR.** "I think women should look at their bodies and *figure out what their assets are* or what they love about themselves," says Lloyd Boston. "Ask yourself, 'Is it my shoulders? My back?' Maybe it's just your ankles. Zone in on one or two amazing areas you always feel good about and choose clothes that celebrate and don't diminish them." Sykes-Rellie adds that you may think of yourself as a certain fashion personality, let's say Bohemian (our No. 5 Fashion Personality), but if tunics and long, flowing skirts make you look too heavy, you may want to express yourself with a unique handbag and shoes.

4. **ASK YOURSELF, "AM I EXCITED?"** When Joan Kaner, the highly professional senior vice president and fashion director of Neiman Marcus, spoke to us about our No. 6 Personality, the Uniform Dresser, she acted like a

kid in a candy store. "It's basic, yet I feel like a million bucks because it's my uniform!" she enthused. *"I feel good in it."* And *Paper*'s Boardman nearly burst through the phone lines when he stumbled on No. 9, Jet Set. "It's not just that I show up in the clothes," he says eagerly, "it's a worldly attitude of confidence and sophistication!" On the other hand, Classic, our No. 1 Personality, nearly put him to sleep.

5. **BE WILLING TO ADAPT.** Do this by asking yourself, "What's my lifestyle?" Then list those situations in which you find yourself on a regular basis— let's say, corporate office, hot dates, spontaneous dinners with friends—and then

Host HINT

Our intrepid *Full Frontal Fashion Top Ten* host Rebecca Budig, an acknowledged Classic, our No. 1 Personality, admits to taking the "feel good" test. If she feels good in what she's wearing, well, then it's a go. And guess what? It almost always reflects her personality and she looks great.

adapt or *refine your personality*, advises Boston. Sykes-Rellie, who is our No. 10 Personality, Mixing It Up, is also a new mom; her lifestyle is more casual now, though her take on casual is still quite glamorous.

6. **REMEMBER: RUNWAY ISN'T REALITY.** Everyone on the fashion circuit knows that what you see on the runways isn't necessarily what you get in the stores. We all know, secretly, that designers really show two collections— one for the press and one for the stores. When one of us spoke to Michael Kors a few years back, he mused, "That's true," and added that he viewed each of the two collections differently: One had TV coverage; the other didn't. The TV clothes, he said, were more provocative; the store clothes were tamer and often already sold to the retailers by the time we saw the runway shows ourselves. Some Fashion Personalities let the runway be their guides more than others (think our No. 3, Fashion Forward) but for the most part we advise you to *go with reality*. As one beauty pro told us this week, don't forget that a lot of those magazine photographs are touched up. Models have got figure flaws just like you, so take the runway with a grain of salt.

7. **GO AHEAD, CHANGE YOUR PERSONALITY!** You're not stuck. Our FFF team member Joan Kaner says that when she retires she plans to become a Bohemian in a long braid, loose, easy caftans, and ethnic jewelry. Elisa Hunter, a friend of ours who is an administrator has gone from "ranch dressing," a more casual take on our No. 2 Personality, Preppy, to seven-hundred-dollar suits that befit a Classic, our No. 1 Personality. Full Frontal Fashion co-host and fashion reporter Christina Ha hasn't quite gotten over the ripped sweatshirts from her intense *Flashdance* phase, and *Glamour's* ultra-stylish executive fashion editor-at-large, Suze Yalof Schwartz (no one loves Manolos more!), says, "I definitely do not dress the same as I did when I was twenty-four and was wearing twelve-inch miniskirts. *Your Fashion Personality can change and it constantly evolves.*"

8. **GET HELP.** The best way we know of to discover or fine-tune your style is to visit the personal shopping department at your local department or specialty store for style advice. Some of us did just that the first time we were invited to the fashion shows in London, Paris, and Milan, and our own co-host and editorial consultant Judy Licht admits, "Most reporters don't have clothing allowances like big stars do, so I would work with one store's shopping service. I learned about my body type and what looks good on me through the eyes of a professional . . . If you don't have a stylist, the best investment you can make is to *find someone who will analyze your look.* You have another set of eyes looking at you and saying what looks good; they don't charge you for the service and as a result, you have fewer things in your closet that you never wear so you end up saving money." The author of this book does it too; it's the best kept secret in fashion.

    > **INSIDER SECRET**
    >
    > Want to know everything, from how to dress for your body type to how to choose the most stylish clothes? Visit the personal shopping department of your local department or specialty store. The service is free of charge and it's like having your own personal stylist.

9. **WE ALL GET LAZY.** As *Paper's* Boardman lamented, even he of the ultra-fashionista males has days when he *just can't be Jet Set*; moreover, he's lazier now, he says, than he was when he was a bit younger. The key to stylish dressing is to be *conscious* of your look; once you are, you can choose to

be lazy—for instance, Boardman's lazy look is an Izod polo shirt and a pair of trusty trousers.

10. **JOIN THE CLUB.** When it comes to fashion, like attracts like. Many of us, consciously or not, dress to signal our membership in a fashion club. Classics pal around with other Classics, Park Avenue Chic's with their fashion crowd, and Eccentrics with the same. You can't miss the black-on-black dress code for Hollywood producers or the handbag-and shoe-of-the-moment for fashion editors. It's like gangs, Boardman says, laughing, albeit style-related ones. Surprisingly, too, many of us also dress exactly like our mothers told us to—without really knowing it. A member of our team actually realized while working on this book that the tweed blazer she felt so uncomfortable in was more the hard-edged style of her high-fashion mom than the more girly look she really wanted. So *realize the connections and be yourself*, fashion-wise.

11. **LIGHTEN UP.** Finally, a word from *Marie Claire*'s wise Sykes-Rellie: *"You shouldn't take fashion too seriously.* It's an added extra. It's the gloss on top of your lipstick. It's the icing on the cake."

Now, read through our list of Top Ten Fashion Personalities and see where you fit in:

CLASSIC

The key characteristics of the Classic Fashion Personality are *timelessness and quality*. You like your clothes to last and care about how they're made; you know and love cashmere; you know the difference between cotton, wool, and rayon blend. You also have a good tailor (or maybe the closest one, for convenience) because you know that with clothes that are more "basic," the most important element is fit.

These days, we're finding two groups of Classics, each stylish in its own way: your mom's Classic, known for twinsets, pearls, and the perfect black sheath

dress (think style icon Audrey Hepburn and the phrase "effortless elegance"), and the newfangled version (think style icon Gwyneth Paltrow), which we're calling Classic with a Twist. So the twinset, the Chanel-style jacket, the baguette bag, the high-heeled boots, the necklace may be worn with a bit more irony, but your jeans are without holes and perfectly and evenly washed.

But Classic does have its pitfalls—or to be more accurate, it has a problem with the pitfalls of others, none more so, say our pros over and over, than even the slightest hint of vulgarity. Says *Glamour's* style guru Suze Yalof Schwartz, who considers herself, as do numerous top-level fashion types, the perfect Classic with a Twist, "Anything that could be interpreted as vulgar is a horror to a Classic."

PREPPY

More than any other Personality, Preppy has the most fashion "flash points"—think barn jackets, ribbon belts, the Bermuda bag, pink and green, Peter Pan collars, the headband, long, flowing skirts, oversized sweaters. It also has its own rules (for example, making sure your collar is standing up or your sweater is neatly tied around your shoulders.) More than any other sign, Preppy indicates membership in a secret fashion club—indeed the clothes themselves do double as country-club clothes.

But much like the Classic Personality, Preppy has now split off into your mom's Preppy—think the famous fashion cues listed above—and the newer version, which is, as celebrity stylist James Aguiar notes, "more imperfect than it used to be." That means newfangled style icons such as Kate Spade (especially her bags!), stores such as Abercrombie & Fitch, and clothing designers such as Lilly Pulitzer. "The new prepster *takes more risks with color*, too," Aguiar continues, "so in addition to pink and green, she might work in another favorite shade."

Preppy has also morphed into Preppy Chic, a stylish look no one captures better than Ralph Lauren (in his top and less pricey lines, too). As Schwartz notes, "You make Preppy Chic by wearing a long-sleeve Polo or Lacoste shirt with white jeans and mules or strappy sandals, or taking a whale-print belt and wearing it with white jeans and a tight sweater, as opposed to an oversized item from a Preppy-oriented catalog." Or as Aguiar suggests, "The modern prepster may wear a denim skirt or a great pair of cropped pants with her Peter Pan–collared shirt."

How does a Prepster run awry? By looking too self-conscious, our style team says. If you're not at ease—let your collar be.

FASHION FORWARD

This Personality is the most confusing because, as our pros well know, the term itself is insider lingo for clothing that is trendy yet appropriate, what experts often call "directional." The True Fashion Forward is *a fashionista who loves clothes*. Unlike the Classic with a Twist, who may fuss over fabric and tinker with a tailor, the True Fashion Forward focuses on fashion: She reads the magazines; she watches style-related TV shows like *Full Frontal Fashion*; she shops 'til she, well, almost drops or at least is done for the afternoon; she has lots of conversations with her best friends about what to buy. As Sykes-Rellie says, this is the Personality that loves creative designers. Her icon of choice is British superstar Alexander McQueen (though she may actually buy approximations of his designs at the store of her choice).

While she buys the latest things—a shirtdress for spring or fall's new tweed jacket—she's never over-the-top or one to throw caution to the wind as is our No. 4 Personality, the Eccentric.

As for missteps, the Fashion Forward's is sporting too many trends. Remember: Fashion Forward is one word away from Fashion Victim.

ECCENTRIC

You know an Eccentric when you see one—think Bjork at the Academy Awards or Sarah Jessica Parker in *Sex and the City* wearing hot pants, a flower, heels, and a seemingly mismatched top. These are the traffic-stoppers and the jaw-droppers, as James Aguiar says. **They wear what they want**, when they want, and they're not afraid of the attention it draws to them. "They're risk-takers but it's who they are," adds Aguiar.

Our style squad member and former *Sex and the City* stylist Rebecca Weinberg is an Eccentric with seventeen tattoos to prove it. Like most Eccentrics, Weinberg doesn't plan ahead (not ever!) or get hot and bothered about dress codes.

The FFF team of insiders knows the fashion industry set of Eccentrics—they include British diva Isabella Blow; her Italian counterpart and audience-stopper at the fashion shows, Anna Piaggi; and the icon of them all, Patricia Field, the star stylist for *Sex and the City*. It is the Eccentrics, our team admits, who sometimes move fashion forward as Field did with that iconic TV show. And there are plenty of them outside the fashion beltway: Cyndi Lauper, Madonna in her "Like a Virgin" days, Gwen Stefani. As for designers, no one beats the pirate-esque John Galliano.

The number-one hallmark of a true Eccentric, though, is her seeming ability to wear hats in public few of us would don in private. The ultimate Eccentric's hat designer is Britain's Philip Treacy. Indeed, late one night we spotted Melissa Muckerman, a twenty-three-year-old club-goer with twenty-five tattoos and twenty-three piercings in pink Docs (she has a preference, she says, for black and pink) and a blonde-and-black seven-inch mohawk held in a cute style with bobby pins (need we say stylish?). As Boardman points out, the Eccentric is always "fun to look at," and "someone you want to hang out with," as another team member notes. As for the clothes, well, we can only guess: A trench coat made from bubble wrap? A seat belt for a belt? Toilet bowl earrings? As Aguiar says, "They do look like they could take their clothes off and it wouldn't matter."

The only blunder you the Eccentric can make is having your appearance serve solely as an advertising campaign for you or your career—then you're not an Eccentric, you're an egocentric.

BOHEMIAN

Bohemian can be a truly beautiful Fashion Personality. It's the sign of the *carefree, free-spirited romantic*: ethnic jewelry; free-flowing hair; hand-embroidered tunics; long, feminine skirts; Ugg boots; and hand-knit pieces (especially now that knitting is au courant).

The best Bohemian, according to our style team members, is a stylish former fashion editor who always looked sleek, chic, and unique in interesting bold jewelry, naturally flowing long, wavy hair and special, often unusual items of clothing from creative designers. As for celebrity icons, our team unanimously voted in Kate Hudson (the daughter of a free spirit), seconded by Liv Tyler (yes, the daughter of yet another); as for designers, well, we nominate fashion designer Anna Sui (Bohemian with a touch of rock 'n' roll thrown in).

Where can the beautiful Bohemian go wrong? Wearing your clothes as a costume instead of a natural outgrowth of your unique personality—in other words, letting them wear you.

THE UNIFORM DRESSER

More than a few of our e-mails are from those of you who would love to know how to dress for less without stress. We do have an answer for you: If you're comfortable with it, the best Fashion Personality for you is the Uniform Dresser. As Neiman Marcus's Joan Kaner indicated, it's the Personality of the great turtleneck, the perfect A-line skirt, the

great pair of crepe pants—in a monochromatic color scheme or neutrals such as charcoal, navy, camel, or brown—dressed up with interesting accessories or even an eye-catching coat or hat. Like the fashion icon the late Jackie O., the Uniform Dresser **blends in and repeats certain basics** while looking stylish and professional.

As Schwartz says, the Uniform Dresser is, "someone who wears the same things over and over again. It could be Helmut Lang or the Gap." (Two great "Uniform" suppliers, we might add.)

Our team nearly burst through the phone lines (yes, they did it again!) when it came to naming icons of Uniform Dressing because the sign includes some of the best-dressed behind-the-scenesters in fashion history: Think Diana Vreeland, the legendary *Vogue* editor-in-chief, known for a simple foundation of high-quality black basics with bold jewelry that set the tone. The late *New York Times* fashion editor Carrie Donovan often sported a simple wardrobe of basics topped off with a standout coat, perhaps in leopard. As you may also notice if you look carefully enough when the world's top designers come out for their bows at the end of their presentations, nearly all of them are Uniform Dressers, none more iconic than Giorgio Armani. He is indeed the king of stylish uniform dressing.

Where can you go wrong? By being boring! Don't forget to have fun with the extras. They don't cost much.

HOT

Hot is the Fashion Personality where warnings rose on our team's radar before everything else because, well, it doesn't take much to go from stylish Hot (what we advise) to too vulgar. In other words, there's a thin line between slutty and sexy. It's an area where, say experts such as *Glamour*'s Schwartz among others, nothing is more important than knowing your body. To be a successful Hot, she advises, you really have know whether your bosom is too big for décolleté or, like Jennifer Lopez, you're small-busted enough so a dress that's low-cut looks chic.

As you can imagine, Hot has icons you can't miss—the designer lines Versace and Roberto Cavalli; and celebrity-wise model Elizabeth Hurley—especially in that memorable Versace dress held together with safety pins. But as our pros noted, *she looked good in it because she knew her body*—the dress fit, there were no too-tight pulls or on-camera yanks or cleavage to her navel.

Hottie styles, our team will tell you, are universal: They include the miniskirt (very tastefully done by the likes of Dolce & Gabbana in their main or less expensive D&G lines—but you can find the stylish look just about anywhere); the halter-style minidress; the low-cut jean; the ultra V-neck dress; and, always, high heels. "The Hot Personality never wears flats," says Aguiar half-jokingly.

PARK AVENUE CHIC

According to our FFF team of pros, Park Avenue Chic is the most label-conscious of Personalities. We don't mean this as a put-down, but rather to say that they wear clothes that send the message to other Park Avenue Chics that they know what true style is. Their trademark is often luxury: multiple-ply cashmere, and as we spotted one recent morning on Park Avenue itself, the perfect Prada anorak, Burberry trench coat, and/or Hermès scarf. Michael Kors stands out, notably for mixing sportier pieces with dressier ones, especially for fancy occasions (PACs receive a lot of invitations to one another's soirees!). We also salute Oscar de la Renta.

The icon of choice for Park Avenue Chic? We nominate the character Charlotte as played by Kristin Davis in *Sex and the City* (after she married into Park Avenue, of course). Estée Lauder's Aerin Lauder is also a stylish standout.

Your most likely faux pas? We say this is the most difficult personality to imitate because luxury is so important—so buyer beware! Maybe you want to begin with one nice piece and then add as you go along—or get thee to your nearest designer outlet mall (see Chapter 8).

JET SET

Paper's Mickey Boardman is, as we said, a die-hard Jet Set. Why, you ask? Because he loves to travel; because he fills his closets with interesting finds from his journeys; and because he considers his Fashion Personality to be one and the same as his lifestyle of fashion-on-the-go.

Jet Set can be ***flashier than other Personalities***; you are the sign of Gucci sunglasses (nothing is more message-sending for a Jet Set than this!); of real fur (not faux, mind you); and lots and lots of Manolos (or, dear readers, of faithful knockoffs anywhere you choose to find them). For the true Jet Set, the axis is often European—New York–L.A.–Paris–London, and, as Boardman adds, Saint Tropez or Aspen. But as Boardman notes, he has lots of friends "with very little money" who simply love to be on the go and pick up great finds.

As to our icon, well, we nominate Tom Ford, the former impresario of Gucci, as much for his former job (Gucci, after all, was known for luggage) as for his own look—the low-hung shirt, the exposed chest, the homes all over the world, and his many TV appearances extolling the jet-setting life. We also nominate P. Diddy. After all, he'll jet in just for a party.

How can you translate Jet Set to your own life? Well, take the style cues, but make sure you don't look too flashy (watch out for hair that is too blonde, our team says!); don't wear too many things that are last season; and if you can't make it to Aspen, well, wear fur to the grocery store instead.

MIXING IT UP

Lots of folks we ran into told us they were the Mixing It Up Personality but the truth is, not as many of us really run interference from one Personality to another with enough comfort to be the real thing. No one on the horizon signifies this better, though, than Sarah Jessica Parker (the person, not the character) who jumps from retro to Eccentric to Classic with a Twist to Park Avenue Chic and back again. She's a fashion gem. The key to her transformation—as it is to anyone who identifies with being a Mixing It Up—is **the confidence to pull it off**. Moreover, as Aguiar adds, as far as style goes, "Instead of being risk-takers, they're more experimental."

They also tend to be skilled at mixing it up outfit to outfit (see Chapter 10, "Become Your Own Stylist"). Think a drugstore undershirt or tank top with Helmut Lang pants, as Schwartz suggests, or Isaac Mizrahi for Target with something from a posh place like Bergdorf's or Barneys or an equivalent spot near you.

What can be the error of the Mixing It Up's ways? Well, being mixed up yourself—by which we mean that you create a "hodgepodge," as *Paper*'s Boardman describes it. So, mix it up if you can do it well; don't if you can't.

10

the top ten

FFF FASHION PERSONALITY DOS AND DON'TS

DO

Keep a scrapbook of your style finds—nothing is more helpful in finding your fashion self.

Find your True Fashion Personality—if you don't, your clothes will wear you.

Know your body type—you can't have a stylish Fashion Personality without this essential understanding.

Fiddle with fit—nothing will make your Personality stand out more (see Chapter 7).

Take the runway with a grain of salt—it's not reality.

DON'T

Be boring—dress up with accessories, no matter what your Personality.

Be Trendzilla—unless you're an Eccentric, keep multiple trends to a minimum.

Be a billboard for your favorite label—one logo is more than enough.

Be vulgar—watch the undercleavage and butt-crack.

Take fashion seriously—have fun, explore, and enjoy the ride!

CAREER COUTURE

Dear Full Frontal Fashion:

I don't have millions to spend on clothes, but boy do I love them.

However, I feel like whenever I go to work (I'm in banking), I have to

wear things that seem really conservative to me. To tell you the truth, I'm

really uncomfortable. What can I do to feel better in my business gear?

TELL ME SOMETHING GOOD

The biggest change in dressing for the office in the last ten years—or, let's say for work in general—is that we work in more varied capacities than ever before (as we invent and reinvent ourselves!) We're banking employees like you, sales associates, schoolteachers, and Web designers. We're in law, medicine, and financial services. And, well, we're also stylists, designers, and TV personalities. Because of this explosion in jobs, the dress codes that made business-dressing so by-the-numbers are no longer applicable.

These days, one job (some of us on the Full Frontal team live this way) can mean several office wardrobes: one for our dressier days (let's say for a client appointment); one for our less dressy ones (when we're with only a few others in the office); one for the outside world (lunch with a client); and one for being altogether casual. How about a latte and a laptop with a colleague, or a job interview at Starbucks?

Let's just say that for some of us it takes more smarts to dress for success than it did to get the job in the first place. Moreover, where a business suit (can we say boring?) used to take us from morning to evening and back again, "Individuality is what gets you noticed these days and it's what gets you ahead," says celebrity stylist James Aguiar. "You don't give yourself up for the job anymore the way corporate drones used to in the old days. There is no uniform anymore." Or as Robert Burke, senior vice president and fashion director, public relations, for Bergdorf Goodman says, "These days, the worst thing you can do is look stiff or rigid."

So how do you detangle the business-dressing dilemma and attempt to dress with some daring, or even create some "eye candy," as celebrity stylist Rebecca Weinberg says—but not so much so that "you oversaturate them with the madness of dressing like a crazy person"? As Burke puts it, a bit more politely, "You want to make a fashion statement without being too bold."

So let us now lead you to the fountain of fashion truth, beginning with our brand-new Top Ten Rules of the Career Couture.

1. **TAKE YOUR FASHION PERSONALITY WITH YOU.** As Aguiar notes, *expressing yourself* is what the new business dressing is all about. Witness our stylish Full Frontal Fashion co-host, Christina Ha. She never goes over the top, but she does wear "something sexy but not showy" (a camisole

and low-slung tailored pants) to work because she wants to feel comfortable at work and otherwise.

2. **REMEMBER: AS YOU DRESS, SO DO YOU ACT.** Neiman Marcus senior vice president and fashion director Joan Kaner warns of the rule of cutting clothing corners—*once you start, you can't stop*: One day you wear jeans and a T-shirt; the next, you don't blow dry; then you're not putting on as much makeup; and before you know it, well, you're acting *differently*. "You have to remember, always, it's a professional situation no matter what your job is, including behind the scenes."

3. **KEEP IT CLEAN.** Author and style expert Lloyd Boston offers a wardrobe warning: So many of us look shiny, polished, and stylish when we're about to get the big job, then six months down the line, "You're dragging yourself into the office in whatever you can grab that morning. The boss never stops looking . . . So ask yourself: Are your shoes shined? Is your handbag the same one you drag to the car wash on the weekend? Has that blouse simply had it from over–dry-cleaning? Is your jacket now shining from too many trips to the same?" If so, *it's time for a wardrobe refresher*.

4. **REFLECT YOUR BOSS.** "He or she should be proud of you and your appearance," says Kaner. "If your boss is conservative," adds Burke, "and you're a little more trendy, you want to calm down your urge to wear trends, maybe add *just a wink of the look* for the moment and then go full-throttle on the weekend."

5. **DRESS FOR THE JOB YOU WANT.** "Dress for *the way you see yourself* in that company," says Aguiar. "If you want to be the head of the corporation, you don't *ever* dress in jeans and a T-shirt." And be sure to look at other people who hold that level job and see how they dress. If they're in suits and you're in jeans, you've just cut way back on your chances of getting the job.

6. **GO AHEAD, OUTDRESS YOUR BOSS.** Advises Boston: Go ahead! Surpass your boss. But make sure you *do it with quality*—for example, a

jacket and trousers or a skirt fashioned from a luxurious fabric; a sweater of the finest-gauge cashmere; a dress from a designer your boss will recognize or admire. But be careful, advises our expert: "You don't want your 'flash appeal' to be brighter than your boss's. You don't want to steal the attention with flashy outfits." "Flashy" is disrespectful because you're out of line with your boss's way of dressing (take another look at item 4 above); and, well, flashy—big jewelry, loud patterns, and so on—is tacky.

7. **CARRIAGE AND POSTURE COUNT.** As our Full Frontal style squad of TV pros can tell you, a great looking on-the-job wardrobe is only 50 percent clothing. "Carriage and posture can *make an inexpensive item look more expensive*," says Boston. "It's very 'don't ask, don't tell.' An inexpensive white blouse worn with the right posture can look like a blouse from Bergdorf's."

8. **NO JACKET REQUIRED.** This could just be the single biggest development in fashion in the last fifty years—a jacket is no longer required on the job. As several of our style pros offered, "A red *sweater* and gray skirt is fine."

9. **BE JUDGED ON YOUR MERITS, NOT YOUR SKIN.** Nothing will make you *appear less serious* (does anyone still say "bimbo"?) than letting your breasts fly, not to mention putting your midriff and tattoos on display.

10. **OPT FOR FEMININE DRESS.** We on the Full Frontal Fashion style squad don't wear bow ties anymore, but we are sending a sartorial signal: Dressing like a man or even mannishly is now passé for a professional. That's not to say a masculine-inspired piece worn from time to time isn't stylish—it is! It's just that the overall look these days is *ladylike*.

THE CORPORATE TYPE

It is possible, dear "Eyeing Me," that you're out of fashion sync with your company's corporate dress code. These days the corporate code can still be somewhat strict, although there's been some loosening up regarding Casual Friday, and a lot fashion-wise if you know how to make your stylish way through the corporate closet.

Dear Full Frontal Fashion:

In my job as a lawyer in Minneapolis, my boss keeps eyeing me as if I'm wearing the wrong clothes, but she never says anything. Should I ask or am I just imagining it? In my old job, my boss was open with me about how she expected her employees to dress. What should I do?

EYEING ME

The real question is, how to begin? If you're not corporate confident, Boston suggests, "Start with the 'holy triumverate' ": a navy blue suit followed by a charcoal gray (medium to dark) and then if you live in a big (can we say dirty?) city like New York, Los Angeles, or Chicago, your third suit can be black. (We do know that some of you aren't permitted to wear pants to the office so in your case the suit needs to be a skirt suit.) Then, be sure to pull the suit apart—the number one no-no among fashionistas these days are clothes that are too "matchy-matchy" or "cookie cutter." Pair the suit with hip, less pricey, and/or more casual items to create a "high-low" look. Try a vintage sweater set, a textured tank top, or a lacy camisole, especially in a super-soft fabric, for an extra touch of chic.

Don't be afraid to buy yourself a fashionable suit to begin with, says *Harper's Bazaar*'s stylish executive fashion and beauty editor, Avril Graham—try one with fuller trousers, for example. Unfortunately, capris, which many of you have asked about, are often nixed by corporate dress codes. The style icon of corporate dressing is undeniably Giorgio Armani and nothing is sleeker and chic-er in the high-powered hallways than one of his great wardrobe signatures: a suit with a featherweight deconstructed jacket that does double duty as a shirt. Try a jacket with decorative stitching and/or a showy lining. Or take Boston's sage advice and buy a less pricey suit or upgrade what you already own with new buttons, "which is something you can do at home while watching TV at night," he says.

Full Frontal Fashion Wardrobe Warning: Your office may have a dual dress code. If you're a lawyer, for instance, the more fashionable jacket may be suitable for the office,

while the more conservative one is what your office's code calls for in the courtroom. In finance, if you're meeting someone in a creative profession, for instance, you can dress more fashionably; if the appointment is with someone from a bank, you're going to have to be more conservative. Even in the fashion business (yes indeed!) folks have been sent home to change.

As you climb the corporate ladder, be sure to augment the quality of your clothing—not only via fabric, but by way of "subliminal or hidden details," as Aguiar says. Examples include pocket detail on a jacket and a subtle drape in the waist or pin-tucking in the back of a dress. Here's another FFF Warning: If you're working your way up, the biggest blunder you can make is logo-dressing. "In the upper corporate world," says Burke, "you should stay away from extremely identifiable items or trends."

Another cutting-edge way to express yourself in dressing for a corporate career is with color—but don't forget to break it up! Color abuse is a corporate catastrophe. "If you're wearing a red jacket," says Kaner, "pair it with a black sweater and skirt. Black tones down the red." And Kaner adds this: "Avoid oversized patterns or loud plaids. It sends a message of flamboyance. Is this a serious-minded person?" According to Sharon Weil, Saks Fifth Avenue's esteemed director of special services (she dresses more Fortune 500 CEOs, socialites, and celebs than most of us will see in a lifetime) loud plaid is, well, against the FFF wardrobe rules when it comes to corporate dress codes.

Accessories-wise, according to Rebecca Weinberg, look for basic black pumps that get their edge from texture. Remember, nothing is more of a "call out" in the corporate corridor than open-toed shoes (and, of course, that staple of our FFF crowd, bare legs).

And never come to work with so much jewelry that you look more like the inside of a department store counter than an employee your boss can count on. Kaner recommends a simple brooch in real or faux gold. As for earrings, Burke says never wear anything that

INSIDER SECRET

If you can't afford Armani, buy a less pricey suit or upgrade one you already own with brand-new buttons. "You can do it at home while watching TV," says author and style expert Lloyd Boston.

makes you look like you're going out for the evening. "Marcasite is a nice substitute for an office situation," says Kaner.

And nothing, but nothing, impresses the boss more than a good watch. If it's cheap and bleak (or has Mickey Mouse on it), leave it at home.

THE CREATIVE TYPE

If you work in a creative career, "the key to dressing is to wear your clothes in a creative way," says Aguiar. "The mix is more important here than it is in corporate life." In addition to obviously having more options, the Creative also has something of an adjunct fashion job: She is meant to be a wardrobe inspiration—not only to herself, but to those who work for her.

So how to do this? We on the FFF style squad say, look for clothes with interesting details— an asymmetrical hemline or interesting pleats on a skirt, for example. Then pair them with your grandmother's sweater and a great lingerie piece underneath. Or wear a unique white shirt by a creative designer like Yohji Yamamoto with perfect jeans and/or a stand-out jacket from a line like Moschino, or a particularly well-tailored one from a style icon like Jil Sander. The equivalent from your favorite store is fine, too.

If jeans are appropriate, Boston and Kaner agree, be sure to buy a great pair of "job jeans." As we write this, Seven is the label of the moment among our style sages, but others will do as long as they fit well, are pressed, are not too low-cut, have an even wash (preferably dark), and always look good with a pair of heels.

You can also have fun with accessories: Pair knee boots with a fave pair of years-old Comme des Garçons or Loehmann's trousers, as Weinberg does, and then switch off to boat shoes depending on the client and the climate. Unlike the Corporate type, you can go hose-less (as our fashion editors do) and even decorate your outfit with something natural like a feather à la Nicole Kidman at the Golden Globes. The decorate-yourself-with-natural-objects idea got a big kick way back when Weinberg and team used flowers in episodes of *Sex and the City* (and it became a trend).

The big blunder for Creatives? "Your work wardrobe outshines your work ethic," says Boston. As a result, adds Kaner, "You don't look reliable."

WORKING AT HOME

"There's a myth that working at home means you can run around in your sweatpants all day," says Aguiar. "You really have to get up and get out, and part of that is getting dressed." As Boston, who worked at home for years, says, your clothes can "send you a message that you're committed."

Our first rule of fashion thumb: Always have a chic work outfit at the ready—just in case. Boston suggests simply buying a suit from one of the "workhorse" stores such as Ann Taylor or Banana Republic or your favorite department or specialty store.

If you happen to slave daily in pj's or beat-up sweats, Kaner suggests asking yourself, "How bothered are you going to be if someone does see you looking like that?" Or, as *Marie Claire*'s Lucy Sykes-Rellie comments, "At home you can look like a slob, the doorbell rings and it's the UPS man, and there goes your future husband."

So you may want to follow the fashion advice of our

intrepid style team member, *Wall Street Journal* Senior Special Writer Teri Agins, who worked at home for fourteen months. She relied on a Nike "uniform" that could easily pass for Prada because it was so chic, what with its black jacket and drapey pants. Aguiar suggests a simple pair of comfortable microfiber trousers with some stretch to them and a cashmere knit top.

And if for some reason you don't have a public outfit on hand or the time to put it on, put on a pair of sunglasses and a quick coat of lipstick and, as Agins will tell you, few will be the wiser.

DAY TO EVENING

Working these days is often an opportunity to become a quick-change artist. Even as we speak, Sharon Weil, our resident expert on what to do from day to evening, is, well, not so sure about her own transition a few days hence for a charity luncheon followed by a party and movie screening sponsored by a major designer later that night. "I'm glad you made me figure it out," she confides.

The easiest way to go from a.m. to p.m. is to wear day clothes that cross the line with a simple change of shoes and/or accessories. We love a simple shift dress or a dressy sweater or sweater

set. Burke suggests looking for one with grosgrain trim or interesting buttons and wearing it to work with a charmeuse skirt. Or try a pantsuit with decorative buttons in the finest or lightest-weight wool you can find and afford. It will also take you from summer to winter.

Day, night, and when hosting our FFF show, Rebecca Budig swears by a pair of chic David Rodriguez capris that have sequins on the pockets.

You can also bring a lightweight beaded or embroidered jacket to work and slip into it later on; or take your work top off and wear the jacket buttoned and by itself.

HostHINT

The cutting edge in day-to-evening wear is dressier outfits that work for day, too. Our host Rebecca Budig wears a pair of David Rodriguez capris with sequins on the pockets. They take her from day to evening, while hosting our FFF show, too.

If you'll be standing at the event, says Boston, always invest in a "signature shoe"; if you'll be seated and only your upper body is on view, consider a jewel-encrusted hair ornament.

And always take a wrap, be it beaded or fur-trimmed. Agins swears by an animal-print pareo she picked up on sale for nine dollars that does double duty as an evening wrap and fits easily in a tote to boot. And no one has ever guessed that it was less than ten dollars, she says (including many a famous fashion insider!).

And don't forget your evening bag (it's what most of us forget, says *Glamour*'s executive fashion editor-at-large, Suze Yalof Schwartz). That's why Agins keeps an emergency kit at work. In it she keeps her favorite bag (a baguette, of course), a curling iron, a complete set of makeup, and an extra pair of heels.

THE JOB INTERVIEW

For a lot of us on the FFF team, preparation for the job interview is a lot like preparing to go on camera, at least wardrobe-wise. Here, our top five rules for winning the get-the-job game:

1. **WEAR NEW CLOTHES.** As Boston notes, "Don't throw out that *'first wear'* on occasions that don't really matter." Remember, a job interview *does* matter.

2. **BUY THE BEST SUIT YOU CAN AFFORD AND HAVE IT TAILORED.** "You can make a two-hundred-dollar suit look like a seven-hundred dollar one if it's *tailored to your body*," says Boston. As to color, we say, navy first, charcoal gray second.

3. **PLAY WITH COLOR IF YOU'RE IN A CRE-ATIVE PROFESSION.** A red suit is fine; so are separates (only one piece, please) in attractive (and often flattering) *shades* such as pink or light blue or even lavender.

4. **GROOMING COMES FIRST.** And gets *noticed first*. Go with a nude nail; minimal makeup; and if your shoes aren't new, have them shined and the heels fixed.

5. **MEMORIZE THE NO-NOS OF THE RECRUITING WORLD.** Claire Julian, a very chic thirty-year-old New York recruiter, says that client companies regularly call her after interviews with this wardrobe query: *"What was she thinking?"* At the top of the list: a shirt with one button too many undone; too much perfume; skirt riding too high on the thigh; big costume jewelry; too many rings, bracelets, or brooches; eyebrows arched almost to the hairline; and, in corporate situations, open-toed shoes. Boston adds to the list: "A bra that doesn't make you feel like a lady. It translates into facial expression," he says. And do avoid overly styled or moussed hair.

THE PUBLIC PRESENTATION

There is no better opportunity, fashion-wise, to wear color than when you're giving a speech or presentation—before a small gathering of friends or in front of a cast of hundreds. Pastels are a particularly fetching choice. "They're more inviting. They open you up and make you accessible and help to carry your word further," says Boston.

Moreover, from a style standpoint, choosing a suit in a pale color makes you "look like a long, tall glass of water," Boston continued. But, as Burke notes, a suit is no longer required. In its place, you may want to consider a floral skirt (or, we add, something in a feminine tweed) with a light-blue sweater set, an interesting jersey wrap dress, and/or a navy skirt with a printed chiffon or silk blouse.

If you're standing at a podium, says Boston, your clothing needs to be more formal. Often this means a jacket. And if pictures are going to be taken, says our friend, hotel executive Kimberly Sundt, make sure your clothes aren't see-through under bright lights.

Not long ago we spotted the perfect stylish public speaker. Diane Mastrorocco, a Weight Watchers leader, was dressed in the perfect brocade suit, its jacket slung open to be consciously welcoming, and underneath it she wore a pink V-neck sweater, at once soft, hip, and stylish.

Finally, a word to the wise from our chic team of TV folk: The jingle-jangle of too much jewelry—if there is a microphone—can cause, well, a retake. And from Weinberg: If you're seeing the same people over and over again, don't double up—at least change your top and your shoes. "I never wear the same thing," says our friend Mastrorocco. "*Never.*"

THE UNEXPECTED INTERVIEW

If you're one of those fashion types who grew up being told by your mom to always put on makeup because you never know who you'll meet, we're saying you never know when you'll meet your next boss.

So a few tips, especially if you work at home:

1. **GO MONOCHROMATIC.** That way you can get out the door in no time. "If you wear two great items from the same color family it will give you *long, clean lines* and help you look like you spent more time getting dressed than you actually did," says Boston. Black or camel is ideal, but if you want to mix two or three shades—say black and red with an accent of white, or camel with another shade, go ahead. Monochromatic is a great travel trick, too (see Chapter 4).

2. **INVEST IN OUTERWEAR.** *Who cares what's underneath* when you're sporting a chic three-quarter-length coat in a bright color, a rich-looking anorak from Prada or one of its copycats, and/or a perfectly fitted featherweight quilted topper with some shine or contrasting fur trim?

3. **PULL YOUR HAIR BACK—TIGHTLY.** It takes two minutes to *fix the flyaways* and that makes all the difference. It's what Burke noticed in a recent job prospect—and yes, she landed the position.

LUNCH OR DINNER WITH THE BOSS

Never change your appearance from your daytime work wardrobe just to have lunch or dinner with your boss. You will send signals that you're either kissing up to him or her or, well, that you have your signals crossed altogether.

If you want to "switch it up," says Aguiar, add a simple high-quality scarf (think Hermès or it's equivalent). And remember: If you can't tie it, don't buy it (as *Harper's Bazaar*'s Avril Graham notes, stores like Hermès offer an instruction card). Or, wear a "nicer" blouse the day of, such as one with French cuffs or a front ruffle and/or a print that is also *très* chic.

But Boston says be wary: Don't assume that lunch or dinner with the boss is the only time "when you're being looked at for bigger and better things . . . you may just be the one in the boss's eye for promotion because someone upstairs just left. Upper management can begin moving the chess pieces before you even know it." So, as we say, you can't lose with a beautiful skirt and that special blouse.

His best advice: Dress in layers. Either build up to a more formal look or peel down to a more casual one—for example, use a sweater set as your base; if the situation with the boss is more casual, wear the cardigan; if dressier, put on the jacket and leave the cardigan behind in your tote.

And, as Weinberg stresses over and over again, "Avoid too much décolletage . . . otherwise he might become your husband or boyfriend. You want to be respected . . . And don't drink too much!"

CASUAL FRIDAY

As much as you may look forward to Casual Friday (if, in fact, your company still has one), our team unanimously says, "use the privilege sparingly"—if at all. As Burke comments, meetings on Friday are just as important as ones on Tuesday and Wednesday.

So what to do if you must? Sak's Sharon Weil says your dress-down day should simply be your sweater set day—with nice trousers. Burke's exception is summer or warm climates where a removed jacket or sleeveless dress is more appropriate.

And Boston warns of what may be the obvious: If you do decide to go more casual, be sure your casual work clothes are not the same as your casual weekend wear. "You don't want to look like you washed the car in them," he says. "They shouldn't be clothes you kick around in." He suggests a blazer, better quality chinos, and nothing higher or lower than a sexy little kitten heel.

And if you're in a creative field, Weinberg says it's OK to go funkier, but not hot. So nix the mini but okay the jeans.

THE BUSINESS OF BEAUTY

On the makeup front, the cardinal rule on the job is don't wear too much. But be FFF warned: You do have to wear some. If you don't wear any, the folks at work may not take you seriously (unless you work at a fashion magazine), so it's really about finding that balance between too heavy and so makeup-less you look inexperienced. For starters, don't get carried away with foundation; stay away from obvious lip liner; don't wear heavy eyeshadow. "You want to look like you've had a nice rest and good vacation but you don't want to look like you're going to a black-tie event," says Bergdorf's Burke.

As for lipstick, stick to the two poles of facial polish—the naturals, including the pinks, or in some careful cases, if you're pulled together, the reds. Avoid purples, browns, or otherwise dark or severe shades.

If you want to update your eyes for evening, says Burke, go smoky rather than flashy; or, as Agins suggests, go with a neutral that has a bit of sparkle to it. Mascara, surprisingly, isn't a requirement.

And our surest-fire tip—if you're not sure about makeup for day or evening, creative or corporate, get thee to a makeup counter, as Agins suggests, and let the experts do you up. It's free and nothing will tell you more about what works—and what doesn't.

And don't forget—nothing beats a great haircut. So, if you're overdue, we say go. Now.

FFF WARDROBE WARNING

Wear minimal makeup to work. If you're not sure about your makeup for the professional arena, no matter the job or situation, get thee to a makeup counter and let the experts do you up, advises *Wall Street Journal* Senior Special Writer Teri Agins. It's free and nothing will tell you more about what works—and what doesn't.

the top ten
FFF CAREER COUTURE DOS AND DON'TS

DO

Invest in your business clothes—one great suit will pay you back—with a higher salary!

Invest in good accessories—especially a watch. Nothing says you're serious quite like it.

Find a good tailor—tailoring can make a two-hundred-dollar suit look like a seven-hundred-dollar one says Lloyd Boston.

Be well groomed—nude nails, neutral lips, and a great haircut land the job.

Keep an emergency kit at work—you'll never forget that evening bag or extra pair of stilettos again.

DON'T

Outflash your boss—yes, we say, do surpass your boss in wardrobe quality—but never with loud patterns or colors.

Overaccessorize—you're a professional, not a Christmas tree.

Be sloppy—this includes over–dry-cleaned clothes and shoes in need of a shine.

Show cleavage—show your bust and, well, that's what could happen to your job.

Wear too much perfume—if the boss uses air freshener, you may need to refresh your résumé.

CHAPTER THREE

RSVP FASHION

Dear Full Frontal Fashion:

I don't get all that many invites, but I received one from a colleague

asking me to "Dress Grand-Tiki Style" for a party she's throwing.

I'm not really the costume type and I definitely don't want to

spend a lot of money on one. Can I go without dressing up?

PERPLEXED ABOUT MY DRESS CODE

feel your event pain! Call it the Invitation Rebellion or the RSVP Blues, but so many of us don't even bother to RSVP so flustered are we by the sartorial requirements. (And no, dear reader, you never *have* to go in costume—your host is not a dress-code drill sergeant!)

In the meantime, though, some of us on the invite-flooded Full Frontal Fashion style team have started to dream about the day when the only code in question is "Anything Goes" and the host really means it. Or, perhaps, "Comfort Zone," or "Comfortable," or "Come As You Are," so if we feel like wearing our favorite jeans and bomber jacket to a Yuletide ball or having our seventeen tattoos on view, well, we can do it. When our gorgeous host, Rebecca Budig, married her husband, an ex-Bachelor from the reality TV series of the same name, she chose to keep her nuptials under wraps so "everyone would be comfortable and they wouldn't have to think about what they were wearing." And our very own celebrity stylist, Rebecca Weinberg, actually gave out a prestigious award at a posh event in a brown leather harness, white suit, and comfy sneakers. "I knew it wasn't appropriate," she said. "But you know what? I had fun!"

So, dear reader, your mom's by-the-book dress codes are truly in the process of breaking down—and pretty badly at that. As a result, there are two things you need to know: 1) Our newfound freedom from by-the-book dress codes means we are now creating more codes than ever before—albeit many of them creative; 2) The new dress-code craziness means that when the invite from the well-intentioned host arrives, all we want to do is throw it out and stay home.

So, let's cut through the code clutter with the only rules you'll ever need (we call them our Top Ten) to RSVP—and, more important, dress in style:

1. **IT'S OK NOT TO GO;** it's not OK to avoid saying so in a timely manner. And, as designer Shoshanna Lonstein Gruss knows (she is invited to at least ten events that involve a stated dress code each month), if the party is "seated," *a timely response is imperative*.

2. **IF YOU DO DECIDE TO ATTEND** a party or event, *go with the code*—you'll have more fun and your host will, too. Remember: A little goes a long way, as we'll soon explain.

3. **IF YOU DON'T KNOW WHAT TO WEAR,** *call or e-mail the host* or the person closest to you who's attending the event—just about everyone does.

4. **DRESS WITH WHAT YOU WANT TO ACHIEVE IN MIND—** whether it be to mingle, network, find a new job, meet your future husband, or support a close friend.

5. **AS *GLAMOUR'S*** executive fashion editor-at-large, Suze Yalof Schwartz explains, if you're not sure what to wear, *don't underdress*. "There's nothing worse than chinos and a T-shirt at a wedding brunch when everyone else is in a suit."

6. **PLAN AHEAD.** Any invite that requires you to *follow a dress code* should arrive four to six weeks prior to the event, to give you time to prepare.

7. **AS REBECCA BUDIG NOTES,** be sure to *respect the host of the party* or event. Budig says that when an event involves older or elderly hosts who may be relatives, she tends to dress more conservatively. Even Weinberg, who has been known to attend a friend's birthday in glow-in-the-dark panties, shows up on our Full Frontal Fashion program in a situation-appropriate skirt and luxe top.

8. **DON'T AGONIZE OR "GET PARALYZED,"** as James Aguiar puts it. "The chic-est women in the world always look as if *they've* never *agonized*," says *Harper's Bazaar*'s executive fashion and beauty editor, Avril Graham.

9. **WHEN IN DOUBT, REMEMBER:** Accessories and makeup may be just about all you need to look code fab—and for very little money, too. There's one FFF accessories rule: As *Accessories* magazine's editor-in-chief Irenka Jakubiak explains, to update your going-out wardrobe, especially an outfit from an earlier fashion season, you *must follow the trends*. "If chandelier earrings are in, they'll update an old party dress one-two-three; if the trend is lace hose or the ribbon belt, then go with that." As for makeup, you may

need to add nothing more than a smoky eye to attend the most anxiety-producing code event in style.

10. **IF THE EVENT IS NEARING AND YOU'RE STILL NOT SURE WHAT TO WEAR,** do follow our advice from Chapter 1 and *get thee to the personal shopping department* of your favorite department or specialty store. There is no better way to cut through the code clutter and walk away in style, no matter your budget or time constraints.

11. **FINALLY, A TOP TEN BONUS RULE:** don't forget, as we've said before, to be yourself. *"Everything depends on your personality,"* continues Jakubiak. "If you're confident about making a bold statement, you could go crazy with a trend; if you're more demure, then you use it singularly." And as Yalof Schwartz adds, "Just because I'm going to a wedding in Texas doesn't mean I'm going to dress like a Texan."

Here, our Top Ten Invitation Dress Codes and the best way we know for you to respond in top-notch style:

WHEN THE INVITATION READS "BUSINESS ATTIRE"

Yes, you can show up in a bland business suit, but we advise just the opposite: Do your best to stand out. As Aguiar says, "You're obviously taken seriously at the office (why else would you be invited to this?). So this is the time to say, 'I'm more than that,' and show a side of you people don't see."

And if you do make a small effort to switch up your wardrobe a bit to look chic, who knows how many top female executives will see you and open the conversation by

remarking, "I love what you're wearing." And we know from our style experience that that seemingly unimportant one-liner might just lead to a new and highly beneficial business relationship.

As businesswomen ourselves, we love the notion of anything that's different and more fashionable than your everyday fare, but can still keep you going into evening, if the event is post-work—think a jacket in white, trimmed in black, or with unique pocket detail (zippers or three pockets instead of two) in place of your everyday corporate uniform. Or, try a suit in a color you don't always wear. We love light gray as an alternative to charcoal, navy, or black, especially when it's layered over a pretty pink V-neck. Or even light blue. (We don't mind a bit of subtle embroidery either.)

And don't forget to switch up your handbag—a slim baguette in a matching shade of pink for the outfit at right would be ideal. Its smaller size and soft color are far more welcoming to potential employers—or dates—than the heavyweight tote you lug around day to day. But do stash your Business Attire bag in the tote the day of the event.

Finally, says Jakubiak, buy yourself some *real* diamonds (or, we say, high-end fakes)—and don't wait for someone else to buy them for you! They're the ultimate Business Attire accessory, offering, as they do, face-brightening to rival makeup—a serious signal to your superiors that prosperity (think big raise!) is no problem for you.

Can you mess up Business Attire–wise? Yes, by not realizing that the Business Attire code is not the same thing as a dance soiree after ten at night. "A party dress and glittery shoes," gulps *Glamour*'s Schwartz. "People would gasp in horror!" Avril Graham agrees: "You don't want to be the Barbie at the business event." And we add this: Play it safe—no open-toed shoes!

WHEN THE INVITATION READS "BUSINESS CASUAL"

The number-one rule of the Business Casual code is to know the nature of the event. Generally, it is a more intimate or dressed-down version of a work-related gathering—often a dinner at a restaurant, cocktails, or, less frequently, a weekend party at someone's house. As Weinberg so wisely notes, this is a great time to loosen up your wardrobe as a sign to your colleagues and clients that they can loosen up, too—all of which can lead to closing the big deal (or opening the door to another).

First off, if you're a Creative type, we suggest wearing a great pair of jeans (see Chapter 4), a designer jacket, and a great mule. For Corporate types, we love a soft sweater (it can have a cowl or turtleneck), a fun top (we love jersey with a drapey collar), or a button-down shirt in a print or pattern and a perfect A-line skirt (we like solid black here if the top is lively).

No matter your job, though, if the location is truly "casual"—we've attended a Business Casual polo match sponsored by a fashion company—a shrunken polo shirt in a color, a turtleneck, or button-front shirt (it doesn't have to be white or light blue) with a high-quality blazer will do, too. You can also pair the top with a full skirt fashioned from a more casual fabric, such as cotton or even fleece. It's a good opportunity, too, to rest your tired stiletto-ed feet in a pair of Chanel-style ballet flats or sleek and trendy driving shoes. And, as Jakubiak suggests, why not sport a stylish straw bag?

WHEN THE INVITATION READS "CREATIVE"

Creative is such a broad moniker that you can wear just about anything, says our team of invite-weary pros. As Graham notes, "Creative is an opportunity for an individual to put her own stamp on it." She also re-emphasizes that it really is "*Anything*. It's adding sparkle; it's adding sequins; it's a Mickey Mouse T-shirt. Literally, it could be *anything*."

So how do you begin—or draw the code line if you see fit? They key for Creative dress codes is the nature of the party itself. As Graham explains, the event itself may be creative. If it's a clambake at the beach, for instance, Graham suggests a great pair of linen pants or jeans with a hip new top from a young designer. Creative means you can also freely sport and support the latest seasonal trend—like a cutting-edge shrunken poncho which, if it's fashioned from a see-through fabric, can be both sexy and sophisticated.

Finally, if you don't have a Creative option in your wardrobe, we say shop for one! One of us recently picked up the perfect Creative option at a designer sample sale—a versatile and spirited sweater in lime green with a black and white border. It's rich-looking; mixes and matches with just about everything; grabs attention because it looks like it's one-of-a-kind; and moves easily from boardroom to beach. Not only that, it's a stylishly respectable conversation opener. You can also go with a suit with a unique and sometimes fun detail such as an unexpected pattern of stripes.

And do also use the Creative code as a time to spotlight your favorite unique and/or handmade accessories. A few weeks ago, we spotted our talented friend, artist Marilyn Fiala, at a code party in a Bohemian-chic beaded necklace fashioned from tiny circles of copper, strung together

with a rich-looking piece of lime-colored crystal on the end. The effect was at once a conversation-opener (we told her how much we loved it and ended up on a rant on her art!) and chic.

WHEN THE INVITATION READS "CASUAL CHIC"

Casual Chic, as Rebecca Weinberg says, really means *upscale* casual. "It's not a handmade dress with hand-painted images from the 1980s. It's sophisticated and appropriate." Or, as Aguiar puts it, "It's understated elegance. These clothes are not the traffic-stoppers." And they are usually worn in upscale surroundings (and likely with a similar crowd) that may or may not involve business associates —for example, a dinner or at-home luncheon, or afternoon holiday or birthday party.

As our FFF team notes, this is when you bring out the great cashmere top, the wonderful designer jacket, the chic pants, and the important blouse or the perfect jean or pant (and we mean *perfect*) with gold shoes and a nice-looking bag. Or consider buying yourself a dress that can be easily dressed up or down (I know we repeat this a lot, but we love the wrap dress); a nice-looking summer sundress works, too. Or look for clothes by a designer known for understated elegance—we vote for Michael Kors (he now has a less expensive line you can consider, too).

In a pinch, Casual Chic can also be, like Creative, more traditional—but if you do opt for a conservative item such as a blazer, make absolutely sure it's well tailored. A member of our style team had one we adored (and frequently wore to "dressy casual" gatherings). It was such a beloved wardrobe staple (it was a Michael Kors) that when she wore it out and found she couldn't replace it, she visited her favorite Hong Kong tailor and had it

copied. She didn't spend much more than it would have cost her to buy a new one; moreover, she was able to throw in a bit of her up-to-the-minute fashion sense via fabric, color, and fit, too (she had it hemmed at just the right spot to cover her "thigh bulge").

Finally, you can only blunder one way when it comes to Casual Chic: by being too casual. Remember: Too casual is not chic.

WHEN THE INVITATION READS "DRESS FESTIVE"

Why is Dress Festive so, well, stress-tive? Why do even our most stylish and invite-mobbed friends and colleagues sigh and say, "I hate that!" Our resident irreverent, Barneys New York Creative Director Simon Doonan, decries the very notion of the label, saying this: If you don't feel festive, why should you *have to*?

On the other hand, Festive does have its time-worn supporters. Designer Shoshanna Lonstein Gruss, of the lively summer wear and skimpy bikinis in oh-so-festive shades of the brightest orange and turquoise, raises a quizzical brow. "What's all the fuss about?" she remarks. "It's just a pair of earrings!"

Dear reader, our buddy Gruss is right, so give up the ghost! Dress Festive is, indeed, a code that, contrary to common thought, doesn't require much (we promise you). It is, indeed, just a pair of earrings; as our own frequent Festive host James Aguiar says, it can also be a pair of fun socks or, as both Aguiar and Jakubiak suggest, wearing a favorite accessory in a nontraditional way—think a brooch or earrings on your shoes; or a polka-dot scarf in your hair. Fabric-wise, it's velvet and brocade; hemline-wise, it's the shortest short or the longest long; embellishment-wise, it's lots

of gold and glitter (on your shoes is fine); and it's the sartorial detail you can picture flying in the wind as you dance up a storm—ruffles, say, or an asymmetrical hemline. It's obviously color, but it doesn't have to be red—and as for your mom's rule (and Schwartz's, too, we add) that it shouldn't be black, well, we spotted a festive beauty at an event a few weeks ago in a bias-cut black dress—her festive addition was a red grosgrain ribbon on her waist.

More than anything, we love the idea of adding "Festive" items to our wardrobes on a daily basis, so that when the moment arrives, all you have to do is show up—but more than that, so we can have fun every single day. "I get a lot of everyday wear out of a satin trench coat," says Graham by example. For *Glamour*'s Schwartz, it's a great green-beaded Fendi bag. Do feel free to add your own take on everyday Festive-ness with, say, a metallic coat or a beaded bag of your own choosing that simply livens up your day (and your night).

A dress you can dance in is also a great wardrobe addition. With that handmade necklace we told you about in the Creative invite section, artist Marilyn Fiala wore a Donna Karan dress with a lively criss-cross of ruffles on the chest and cool Cynthia Rowley shoes with a similarly striking criss-cross design to a Festive charity benefit. And do note, dear reader, that she was a smart Festive shopper: She also wore her Festive dress to her sister-in-law's dockside wedding and plans to sport it on an upcoming trip to Los Angeles in more casual settings, with a pair of sexy sandals. And we're not done yet—the somewhat see-through dress is worn with a slip dress underneath, which Fiala also plans to wear by itself to fun parties after ten at night.

If you're getting into it now (I know we are!), we also suggest adding a fun suit to your Festive shopping basket and then wearing it to work or to Business Attire events or even a cocktail party—we love one we spotted the other day on a TV colleague in man-tailored glen plaid with a subtle sparkle and more feminine light-pink trim.

Finally, if you do want to be daring, this is the opportunity to don that one item (vintage is more than fine) that you never throw out but never quite muster the guts to wear. One of us has a show-stopper we picked up on Carnaby Street in the 1960s—black and floor length, it has faucets at the nipples and bright streams of color coming down from there to the floor. Aguiar, of course, says he'll throw a Festive party celebrating it.

(Carnaby Code anyone?) One stylish waitress we came across told us she has a favorite "weird hat" that she always puts on in front of the mirror and then takes off the second she leaves her apartment so fearful is she of the appraisals of others. We're here to say, this is the moment to set yourself free!

Schwartz won't let us finish until she gives you her emergency answer to the festive-ities: You can always pick up a turquoise boa at a store like Ann Taylor, she says. If every-one in the room is dressed Festive, keep it on; if they're ignoring the code, feel free to stash it and have fun anyway.

WHEN YOU NEED A GRADUATE DEGREE TO DECODE IT

We've gotten them—the Dress Poisonous; Dress Heavy Metal; Dress to Sparkle; Dress Moody; Dress Nautical Chic (for boat parties); Dress Black; Cowboy Attire; Red, White, and Blue; Black and White; Summer Barbecue; and Summer Black Tie—the seemingly oddball barrage of invite codes that give us a bad case of code confusion—or at least require a visit to a really good personal shopper to figure it all out. But who has the time, anyway? Don't we women have more important things going on?

Well, we're here to cut through the code confusion and tell you that nearly 100 percent of such codes are for theme parties for birthdays or holidays—from the Fourth of July to Halloween. And just like our Dress Festive advice to you, let it be known that you don't have to do much at all.

Our very own Aguiar, for instance, hosted a July Fourth event with that dress code of red, white, and blue. "It doesn't mean you have to come dressed like the flag," he says, "it can just be a bandanna or a pair of jeans." For that Heavy Metal invite, Gruss simply cov-ered her arms with rubber bracelets (afterward, dear reader, she found what we found out, too—that all of you who showed up theme-less "were jealous" and asked to borrow a few!

Dear reader, that Grand-Tiki Style party? We say go with a simple lei and, if you have time, pick up a Hawaiian shirt.

Finally, you can always go with the easiest and most effortless thematic mainstay, makeup. For Dress Poisonous, Gruss gave herself vampire-like smokey eyes; for Dress to Sparkle, she covered her upper lids with glittery shadow. You can also have fun with hair. For Heavy Metal, all Gruss did was tease it.

The only Full Frontal faux pas, as Gruss (who entertains a lot) says, is being too cool to dress up. "It's insulting to your host," says Aguiar.

WHEN THE INVITATION READS "COCKTAILS" OR "COCKTAIL WEAR"

We say, forget your grandmother's or even your mother's boring black cocktail dress and go with something *a lot* more cutting edge by going with the "dress" in dress code. Our only rule is, keep it ladylike—think a colorful sheath with interesting detail; a chiffon dress in a fun color or style. One stylish woman we know just received a top honor at a fancy New York hotel—dress code Cocktails. With everyone else in boring business wear, she sported a hippie-chic Chloé dress that not only set her apart from everyone else but made her a respectable sartorial role model. A backup? A blouse and skirt that give off the same effect.

And if the occasion is a special one for you, this could just be the perfect time to try the trick some of our own style

team members use (and keep quite secret)—borrow a dress. Our friend in the Chloé did just that (from a fashionista colleague)—she looked chic and saved $1,000-plus in the process.

As for accessories, go for those that fit in with the fact that you're likely to be on your feet, perhaps with a drink in your hand—a colorful wrist clutch is great, as is that must-of-musts, comfy shoes—try sexy ones with a lower Louis heel. It's the perfect cutting-edge footwear for ladylike events such as this one, in addition to the low-heeled kitten heels or mules you may already have.

THE WEDDING PARTY INVITATION

When it comes to wedding party invites, our pros say the number-one consideration needs to be your destination. If you're going to travel, know that your clothes need to be travel-ready—leave the poufs at home and go for wrinkle-proof fabrics (we like silk jersey and chiffon). And know that this is the one exception to the Top Ten Travel Rules in Chapter 4: Start your pack list at least three-plus weeks in advance and your shopping (if you have any to do) at least two.

Now we take you to the rehearsal dinner. And, as Aguiar notes, this is the time to lowball it—you've just gotten off the plane or out of the car and the last thing you want to do is make a big deal over your dress. The ideal rehearsal wardrobe is the suit you wear to work; a nice pair of pants with a good-looking jacket, silk blouse, camisole, or sweater, and a good-looking shoe.

For the post-wedding brunch, however, we advise doing just the opposite—switch up your wardrobe because you're now taking part in an extension of the wedding. This is not brunch with your buddies at your

favorite hangout in your hometown or city. Our number-one pick is a special pleated skirt and a jersey top with a draped neckline, a sleek bag, and stylish shoes. If the outfit is new, it's even more of a respectful sign to the bride. And whatever you do, take the time to blow-dry your hair or put it up stylishly (if you need a forty-five-minute appointment with a hotel hairstylist, make it!) no matter how late you got in from the festivities.

Finally, if you're a bridesmaid, Aguiar says, you no longer have to put up with a color scheme or style of dress that you don't like, can't afford, or that makes you look like a blimp on fire—but you do have to keep in mind that the "maid" in bridesmaid means just that. The cutting-edge etiquette experts on our FFF team say the au courant action is to get together with the other bridesmaids, decide on a color scheme and style of dress that suits all of your ages and body types, then arrange to confer with the bride (or one of her representatives if the event is big). One of the most stylish weddings we've attended to date took place ocean-side. In place of the original gray scheme suggested by the bride, the group offered up a variety of hues in the blue family. Each woman would buy her own dress, length mid-calf or longer. The result? From the deck chairs, the wedding party resembled a Gauguin painting (and looked equally amazing in photos).

Accessories-wise, says Jakubiak, the bridesmaids' "committee" can also suggest a group "statement piece"—for instance, a necklace or long earrings. Just make sure you only have one statement piece, and that your other baubles are minimized.

When you do shop for that dress, our nouveau etiquette also says it's more than OK to buy one that you can wear again and again. That's why black is so popular these days. As Graham notes, "Now bridesmaids' dresses are not quite the awful things they used to be. They can often do double duty, especially as a black-tie option, if the dress isn't all ribbons and bows and the awful things bridesmaids' dresses used to be." One great way to do that is not to limit your search to the bridal industry. As we noted, our stylish friend Marilyn Fiala wore her ruffled navy-blue mid-calf Donna Karan from Dress Festive for her wedding party role and looked fantastic.

The only blunder we know of at FFF is worrying about your wedding party wardrobe. "Speak up," says Aguiar. "This is not the Dark Ages."

THE WEDDING INVITATION

Wedding dress codes are frazzling as quickly as the hems on our favorite old jeans. There are a few considerations, however, that never go out of style: 1) Don't outshine the bride. This is her day, not yours, so hold your fashion breath if you want all eyes to turn in your direction. 2) Don't wear white. Yes, rules are fading fast, but this move can equal if not outshine the bride, so why bother? 3) As for black, it used to be considered bad luck, but these days, well, it's in style. 4) Consider the crowd. "If it's my best friend from high school," says Schwartz, "I can dress more festively. If it's my husband's boss, I need to be more conservative." 5) Consider the vibe. As Doonan notes, ask yourself, is it bohemian or more traditional? 6) Don't forget the weather. "You don't want to be in a strappy dress in the freezing cold," says Schwartz. Graham suggests wearing an outfit with a jacket you can easily remove. 7) Wrap it up. Whatever you wear must take you from church or temple to reception and/or the wedding itself. It's OK to wear a strapless party dress (as we will soon explain), but be sure to cover yourself with an appropriate wrap. 8) Always look to your destination for style clues. "If it's New York, I might wear a black dress," says Schwartz. "In Washington, D.C., I might go for a suit." As we explained, that doesn't mean throwing your personality to the wind— it means adapting it. If you're more of a Fashion Forward type, wear a trendier suit. 9) With weddings in particular, you may always want to ask your host or a friend for advice as a safety—I know we do. For bigger affairs, someone may be designated to help you in the bride's absence. 10) Assess before you invest. If you go to a lot of weddings, you may want to buy something new that you

can use over and over again; if you don't, you may want to start looking for dresses that are versatile enough to go from wedding to other events in your life. Or, as we noted earlier, you might want to borrow something.

So what are your wedding options? To be very honest with you, dressing for a wedding is not the big deal it was in your mom's day. It requires nothing more than a party dress that you can find within blocks of your home in any price range you choose. If the code is black-tie, it can be, in many cases, long or short (be sure to ask); and, if it is long, it can be a wonderful column, bias-cut, or off-the-shoulder style, all of which flatter most body types. For a less dressy wedding (black-tie optional fits in here), just go with a versatile party dress. We love strapless styles with a bit of roominess in the skirt (if you're not comfortable with your arms, go with a stylish bolero or a wrap).

And whether your dress is long or short, column or strapless, the style will be in the details—ruching, gathering, fabric inserts, or flounces; beading, draping, sequins, embroidery; corsetry details; jeweled straps and jewels on the straps; covered buttons; a subtle pattern like a rose-print brocade or a crocodile print on silk or satin; toga, halter, and one-shouldered styles.

You also have a wide choice of fabric. Chiffon and silk jersey are good choices, as is satin, although it may be a bit less forgiving. Be sure to check yourself out in a three-way mirror.

Finally, accessories are what make your wedding dress pop. And nothing is more important than how you balance them (as we noted, one show piece or trend is enough). With our favorite little strapless party dress, *Accessories* editor Jakubiak recommends putting your hair up with jeweled ornaments (if you have the hair for it) and then maybe adding a cuff bracelet; if not, opt for long, showy earrings and skip the necklace. For a V-neck, for example, we love a Y-shaped necklace as the show piece (it's OK for its pendant to slip into your cleavage) and then just a simple pair of studs (nothing more). For a simple column with a small circle of a neckline, you may want to show off a choker and not much else; and for a scoop neck, if your show piece is a necklace, be sure you choose one that's also round and stops above the neckline, then downplay the earrings or opt for studs.

Short or long dress, you always want to carry a silk, satin, or jeweled bag. It's proper from our FFF style standpoint. As for that wrap, even if you're not invited to the ceremony itself, take it with you, because our experience tells us your wedding setting will either be over-airconditioned or the summer weather will suddenly be on hiatus for the day.

Our only FFF Warning: Avoid screaming florals and anything with miles of cleavage—especially if you're going to the church or temple first.

THE BLACK-TIE AFFAIR (OR IS IT?)

Black tie is likely the most controversial of dress codes. Even on our own stylish team, we have the purists who say if the invite says "Black Tie," you wear a gown; if not (say, "Black Tie Optional") it's OK to go short. We, however, are followers of the newfangled etiquette which says short (not mini) is fine, unless it's what we're calling "real black tie." Our glamorous host, Ms. Budig, wears a short dress to all black-tie dress code affairs, with the exception of the Emmy Awards, where she wears something long and very dressy. And if being the only short in a sea of long or the reverse bothers you, make sure you find out what the crowd is doing before you shop.

For Black Tie Optional dress codes (which, by the way, our team of style pros wish didn't exist in the first place; if you want your guests to dress in a certain way, why not just say so rather than giving them so many choices they end up suffering from dress duress?), we love the idea of a dress by a designer who is not necessarily a traditional mainstay of black tie—Catherine Malandrino comes to mind or Tuleh or even Karl Lagerfeld for H&M (we found a great gown for under a hundred dollars at a similar store). We also like evening skirts in chiffon—we spotted one recently that has moving panels (it's an interpretation of an old Lagerfeld) and looks chic and sexy with everything from a sleeveless cashmere turtleneck and pair of fabulous gold earrings to a short-sleeve T-shirt from the Gap (remember Sharon Stone at the Oscars?).

As for Black Tie itself, if you're going with short, our wedding-party list in the previous section is ideal. But if you're opting for floor length, we do recommend a one-piece dress; while two-piece numbers are very popular because you can pull them apart in no time, many of the women we've observed at our many black-tie events just blend into the background. The message is, "I somehow managed to do just enough to get through the door."

Finally, do remember that gowns these days are not what they used to be—don't think that because a dress is floor length it can't take you from wedding to other occasions. One member of our illustrious team owns a perfect one from designer Isabel Toledo. Fashioned from soft, flowing black jersey, it has a creatively draped bodice and a ballerina-style skirt that both hugs the body when she stands still and swirls around in a flirty motion when she moves. It's fancy enough for all black-tie codes and works just as easily for gallery openings and holiday parties. It's also truly comfortable, that all too rare quality we definitely want you to look for in any evening clothes you buy.

As for the perfect accessories, follow our "one statement piece" rule in the wedding section; it's one and the same for Black Tie. You can definitely wear the same dress, bag, and baubles to both (and then some).

10

the top ten
FFF RSVP FASHION DOS AND DON'TS

DO

Buy a dressy dress—a gown and/or a great party dress is what equals success.

Follow the dress code—otherwise, you may insult your host.

Make a splash—it's OK to outshine everyone on your RSVP list—except the bride.

Buy a fun and feminine suit—it will take you from business attire to cocktails to holiday gathering to fancy date and back again.

Avoid underdressing—if you're not sure, give yourself a little more.

DON'T

Forget to RSVP—it's OK not to go—just be sure you say so.

Stress over your dress—call the host or a friend; we all do!

Wait 'til the last minute—a well-planned entrance is worth the effort; that's why invites are sent four to six weeks in advance.

Under-accessorize—too few baubles or a boring bag can a wallflower make.

Be flashy or vulgar—you don't want to be the one everyone gossips about afterward.

CHAPTER FOUR

GORGEOUS
GETAWAYS

Dear Full Frontal Fashion:

I'm a real tacky traveler and don't own nice things. I travel in sneaks,

jeans, and glasses so my contacts don't dry out. I also use obnox-

iously faux luggage that my in-laws treated me to. Please help!

TACKY IN NEW YORK

Traveling in style can be as frustrating as editing your closet— you always have the best of intentions and then, whoops!, you find you can't let go of those ten pairs of black pants or six sets of your favorite heels, or you're not sure whether you'll need twenty different outfits for the trip in Mexico—so you pack everything and end up spending every single day in a bathing suit. Or you get to your destination and guess what? Three unexpected occasions crop up, one of them dressy, and you forgot to bring even the tiniest shred of anything fancy. Or perhaps your luggage was lost or delayed in transit to the Dominican Republic and you're stuck in jeans for four days because the resort doesn't have a shop, and even if it did, you don't have the money to invest in a whole new wardrobe.

Well, these are all true tales of travel woe from our expert team of styling pros. And yes, traveling out of style happens to best of us world-weary voyagers. Lucy Sykes-Rellie, the editor-at-large at _Marie Claire_, has learned a lot since the days when she could singlehandedly have inaugurated the first chapter of Overpackers Anonymous with the "massive trunk" she lugged up four flights to the room where she stays while visiting her close friend in London. "It was like a coffin," she recalls. "It was bigger than me!"

So how can you be a truly gorgeous traveler? Supremely destination-chic? Hot 'til you drop when you're away from home? Well, for starters, listen to celebrity stylist James Aguiar, a member of our far-reaching, world-traveling Full Frontal Fashion style team, who says so smartly, **_"When you travel, you definitely have to drop your Fashion Personality!"_**

Lucy Sykes-Rellie's take on it is similar: At home she wakes up and dresses to fit each day's mood. On the road, however, "You can't play with your moods!" That's why Laura Begley, style director of _Travel + Leisure_ magazine, admits she sometimes feels sad on the road—she's wardrobe displaced. Or as _Town & Country_ editor-in-chief Pamela Fiori puts it, separation from our everyday wardrobe can cause insecurity.

But there is hope! As our most stylish, roving FFF team members have found, yes, we've had Pack Attacks, too, but we've also discovered oh-so-chic solutions. It takes practice, mind you! Designer Diane Von Furstenberg, who describes herself as one of the best packers in the world (she says she designs everything with travel in mind), puts it this way: "You'll find that packing is good training for life because it forces you to think through

what you need and don't need and put it together in an organized way. Traveling and packing is total training for life in general!"

So here's a step-by-step plan for the perfect stylish journey, beginning with the all-important, often overlooked, Pre-Trip:

1. **PLAN AHEAD.** If you want to travel in true style, our team says don't ever wait until the last minute. ***Begin the packing process three days before*** you leave; identify the situations you expect to find yourself in—and those you don't (a late arrival, perhaps, or an unexpected event)—and then picture what you're going to wear to each one. As Pamela Fiori says, "You don't just throw things in a bag. You think about what you're going to be doing on your trip. Is it a business trip? Is it a trip with a lot of events in the evening? Are you going to be outdoors and trekking around with mud and soft grass? All of those things come into play."

   "Prepare for all situations so you don't wear yourself out during the travel process," urges *Travel + Leisure*'s Begley. To keep track of it all, Lucy Sykes-Rellie takes a "mental Polaroid" of her outfits; still other Full Frontal Fashion pros actually take Polaroids. We suggest writing everything down.

   > ### FFF WARDROBE WARNING
   > If you haven't worn it in two years, don't take it. And new doesn't mean better; if the old shoe fits, is appropriate, and you love it, take it. And be sure to do any wardrobe research before you leave: We recently ran across Therese Holm, a veteran flight attendant with a lot of on-the-road style who admits she found herself, well, culturally clueless—she was turned away from Vatican City because she was wearing a sleeveless shirt.

2. **LIVE IN LAYERS.** We recently spotted Iris Gergis, a twenty-something copy shop employee, in our favorite travel combo: a featherweight black cotton cardigan with a flash of lace at the V-neck peeking out. With no muss or fuss she looked good to go—anywhere in the world, day or night or in-between, with her choice of bottom. Everything you pack needs to layer over or under everything else, and the best way to do this is by ***embracing your neutrals***, preferably a chic foundation of colors based on black, camel, khaki, cream, and/or white (after that you can always add in occasional

Live in Layers. Our favorite layering combo?

A simple, sleek cotton cardigan over a go-anywhere

sexy camisole.

Know Your Neutrals.

The perfect travel wardrobe is a mix

of black, camel, cream, and white,

says *Glamour* magazine's Suze Yalof

Schwartz.

items in accent colors like red, blue, or even lime green and/or hot pink). Living in neutrals allows you to create the maximum number of outfits without repeating yourself. It's the only color scheme *Glamour* magazine's executive fashion editor-at-large Suze Yalof Schwartz adheres to.

3. **FILL IN THE GAPS.** *Now.* If you need to complete your travel wardrobe, *do it before you leave town*—unless you're sure you'll have plenty of leisure time to shop (for instance, on a beach vacation) and that the item isn't important anyway.

4. **LIGHTEN UP.** Do this in terms of fabrics. We love seasonless clothes fashioned from year-round fabrics such as silk, silk jersey, lightweight cashmere, super-lightweight wools, lightweight wool crepes, and clothes that are branded "microfiber" and "wrinkle free." It's a good idea to *buy seasonless clothes* whenever you shop so you always have a travel-ready wardrobe in place (we do). You also want to lighten up the bag(s) you carry. We on the FFF roving style team take one small piece of luggage and a carry-on. We never check baggage! If you need to take more, Schwartz recommends a garment bag so you don't have to bother pressing or unpacking when you reach your destination. Never pack anything you'd be upset about losing. "One out of every ten trips I'm on my luggage goes missing," warns Begley. Sykes-Rellie still recalls the reaction of a close friend who took her best pair of suede trousers on a wedding weekend only to have someone spill a margarita all over them. And always, always take your toiletries with you on the plane. "These are your security blankets," emphasizes *Self* fashion director Evyan Metzner. "I'm shocked when people check them!"

5. **KEEP A PACK LIST.** Write down everything you're taking for every trip and situation within that trip. Edit as you go.

6. **KEEP A TRAVEL DRAWER.** If you travel a lot (or even if you don't), dedicate a separate drawer to travel. In it, our FFF team strongly recommends *keeping a second set* of your favorite toiletries in travel-sized containers— shampoo, moisturizer, conditioner, your favorite fragrance(s)—in Ziploc bags. Some of our Full Frontal Fashion pros then put the Ziplocs inside cosmetic

bags because they've experienced numerous inside-the-suitcase spills. Jennifer Cattaui, a stylish world-traveling fashion editor, keeps brand-new Petit Bateau T-shirts at the ready in their original paper-thin boxes. Celebrity jewelry designer Ippolita Rostagno (with clients including Kate Hudson, Debra Messing, and Courteney Cox) is ready to roll in another way. She keeps a second set of outfits ready to go in their dry-cleaning bags (to prevent wrinkles). Moreover, she says, if your outfits are clean and ready to go, you'll be more likely to take them with you and won't be tempted to overpack. Keep your pack list(s) in your travel drawer, too.

PACKING THE PERFECT SUITCASE

The foundation of on-the-road style is a perfectly packed suitcase. Like a great meal in a four-star restaurant, it's all about mixing and matching the perfect five-star ingredients. Without exception, our Full Frontal Fashion team consider the following your travel must-haves:

1. **SLEEK BLACK PANTS IN A CHIC, TRAVEL-READY FABRIC.** We love them in lightweight crepe with a bit of sheen; in a dressier satin with a low-luster shine; in a cool tuxedo style with more subtle detailing. *Dress them up or down*; buy them just about anywhere.

2. **A DIGNIFIED PENCIL SKIRT HEMMED AT THE KNEE.** We suggest black, but feel free to go with your favorite neutral (we love camel, too). Suze Yalof Schwartz never leaves home without her version in silk jersey by Calvin Klein. If you have a fuller figure, you may want to pack an A-line skirt in a neutral shade or just a basic skirt that you feel good in.

3. **A BLACK SHIFT DRESS.** Wear it under a jacket or cardigan or shawl; for business, vacation, or hot date; *doll it up or tone it down*. Avoid linen.

Pack the Perfect Suitcase.

Packing the perfect suitcase
is like a great meal at a
four-star restaurant: It's all
about mixing and matching
the right ingredients.

4. **AN EVENING SKIRT FASHIONED FROM A SHEER FABRIC.**
We love chiffon; and *wearing it with everything*: a cute fitted Tee (for a party); a simple white cotton shirt or satin blouse (for cocktails); a jacket (for a business dinner); a decorative lace or embroidered top (for dressier situations). When *Self's* Metzner turned twenty-six, her then-boyfriend sent her a "ransom note" telling her where to show up for what would turn out to be a surprise romantic weekend. She decided to "splash out" and bring something dressy: a sexy lace skirt (unlike a silk one, she says, she could roll it up into a ball). In Barbados recently, she packed her favorite gauze skirt. We also love evening skirts with a sleeveless black cashmere turtleneck that can then do double or triple duty with trousers, skirts, or even jeans.

5. **FOUR TOPS.** As *Glamour's* Suze Yalof Schwartz and many of our world-weary pros insist, always pack at least four tops (*a minimum of two for every bottom*). We suggest a great fitted T-shirt; a lightweight, short-sleeved knit (cashmere is ideal); a basic camisole; and a boffo blouse in a fun color, print, pattern, or interesting fabric design. Designer Stella McCartney is known for the latter but you can find them anywhere. Designer Ippolita, who has gone around the world in the last six months, says she used to consider any blouse over thirty dollars a rip-off until she discovered a lively two-hundred-dollar flower-child-style topper from designer Anna Sui and made it her on-the-road staple. "It was worth every penny," she says. And feel free to be creative: Not long ago we spotted Angela Carton, a college student from Chicago, on a train to Washington, D.C. She was sporting a perfect sleeveless pleated-style top from Kenneth Cole; she wore hers with jeans but it works beautifully with every bottom in your suitcase; it won't wrinkle, and rolls up into a ball.

6. **A LIGHTWEIGHT, CASHMERE V-NECK IN A SOFT COLOR.** It *works with everything* for day; keeps you warm; always looks chic; and surpasses the latest runway trends.

7. **A SHRUNKEN BLAZER.** We consider a basic blazer with a bit of fashion to it—in this case, a slightly smaller, *fitted shape*—to be the stylish topper for every travel situation: plane, car, train, city, country, day, or evening. Don't leave home without it.

7. **THREE PAIRS OF SHOES (AND WEAR ONE!).** "I've taken twenty pairs of shoes with me to Paris," muses Lucy Sykes-Rellie. "Oh my God! What should I wear? What should I wear? And I end up wearing the same two or three pairs. *Take the absolutely fabulous things you wear all the time.* They're your favorite friends at that moment." Take one pair of dressy heels, one pair of comfortable, smart-looking shoes, and boots if you're taking part in an outdoor activity that requires them; and always wear the heaviest shoes on your trip.

FFF WARDROBE WARNING

Beware of beaded tops . . . they can snag and catch on your travel wardrobe. Instead, we recommend a pleated top like this classic from Issey Miyake.

PLAYING THE PLANE GAME

Overdressed is better than underdressed, even if everyone around you looks as if they're going to a baseball game, the gym, or they've slept in their clothes. As *Glamour*'s style guru Suze Yalof Schwartz puts it, "I don't care if you're twenty-three or seventy-five, you should always dress up when you travel because you just never know who you'll bump into . . . It could be the ex you were hoping to bump into, the one that got away. It could be your next boss, your future husband, all of which deserve the same amount of attention to wardrobe detail." And you'll also have a better chance of an upgrade.

The best way to play the plane game is go monochromatic. Wear head-to-toe black and your wardrobe won't show stains or wrinkles when you disembark. A pashmina (we love pale pastels) will do wonders as a wrap to keep you warm on the plane (*Self*'s Metzner is not alone in describing herself as feeling "cryogenically frozen" on air-conditioned planes) and also serve as a blanket now that more and more flights don't offer them. Our host Rebecca swears by her special pashmina by designer Sonya Madden—a true travel find, it has sleeves so that Budig's arms are free.

As for shoes, our friend Suze Yalof Schwartz may tiptoe through the airport in Manolos but we suggest an easy pair of shoes that combine comfort, function, and fashion. Opt for a pair of Chanel-style ballet flats or black loafers. "Your feet puff up and then you try to squeeze them into Manolos!" says Sykes-Rellie, who prefers Christian Dior sneakers. She also notes that you may not want to find yourself running around the local convention center in stilettos, should your luggage be delayed. You may also want to pack a pair of slippers with rubber soles—you can slip them on in flight and also to tiptoe through the metal detectors so your feet won't touch the airport floor.

For a stylish business trip, the items in our suitcase work beautifully. Here are a few other things you may want to consider: *Glamour*'s Schwartz is a skirt-a-holic. "Skirts are key. They're possibly the most important element in your business wardrobe because in a skirt you always look dressed and ready to conquer." She packs three, all pencil skirts, in neutrals (black, camel, cream). For dressier occasions, be sure to include a top in a metallic fabric, or one with embroidery. And celebrity stylist James Aguiar strongly advises, "Always bring a chic carry-on bag that doubles as a super-size handbag and remember to put a change of clothing and your toiletries in it just in case your flight is delayed or your luggage is lost." We love the bags fashioned from fake croc in fun, bright colors; they're easy to find at nearly all your favorite stores. And finally, don't forget to take at least one white shirt in either cotton or satin or, better yet, a stain- and wrinkle-free

INSIDER SECRET

Fashion editor Jennifer Cattaui was eating dinner at a posh Paris eatery when someone spilled red wine all over her crisp white shirt. Thank goodness it was this wrinkle-free, stain-free find from Samsonite. The wine beaded off with barely any effort.

fabric that's also stylish. "If you're looking tired and off color, you put it on and boom! It zings you!" says Sykes-Rellie. Of course you always want to pack gym clothes if you work out or want to go for a run, and/or a bathing suit. A member of our intrepid team actually once brought a bathing suit to Switzerland in winter just in case she needed one!

If your trip is more casual, adapt like Diane von Furstenberg does and bring a leather jacket instead of a shrunken blazer. If, like she does, you also have formal occasions on your itinerary, please don't bring a ballgown! Follow her lead (and our perfect

suitcase) by wearing a dressy skirt or trousers in a lightweight fabric, and a glamorous top.

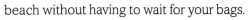

For that va-va-voom vacation getaway, we subscribe to the Dress Theory of Life. As *Glamour*'s style guru says, this is the time to feel ultra-sexy. No exceptions. Pack a dress for every day. And make it a big Wow! The travel winner is undoubtedly the wrap dress created by Diane von Furstenberg. All our pros say to take at least two bathing suits and be sure to put them in your carry-on so you can go to the pool or beach without having to wait for your bags.

Aguiar says stick to two styles: a one-piece halter and/or a bikini if that's your style (remember: leave trendy styles at home!). Then pair the halter with a wardrobe of sarongs and wear the outfit at breakfast, beach, lunch, dinner, and, well, even at night with a brooch or flower pin. And you can always use the sarong as a towel or blanket on the beach, too. Finally, be sure to include a pair of flip-flops and a pair of the metallic sandals of the season (we like them strappy) in your carry-on!

For a more adventurous journey, you might be surprised that we suggest sticking with our suitcase basics with just a few simple tweaks. For colder climes, *Town & Country* editor-in-chief (and adventure traveler: think African game camps) Pamela Fiori is always game in a stylish quilted parka. She also wears it in the city and back home—in fact, she bought her entire wardrobe for a trip to India at Banana Republic. Look for a version of the quilted jacket in a fun color or pattern with a lean fit so you don't end up looking like an oversized sausage or a big balloon. You can also invest in a rich-looking vest (Ralph Lauren does beautiful ones); we love them in suede with a sleek knit collar over a cashmere turtleneck. If your trip is more adventurous, says Fiori, think shorts, khakis, or chinos, cotton turtlenecks, waterproof boots, gloves, and clothes with lots of pockets. As for hiking boots, Laura Begley takes old ones to the Swiss Alps and leaves them there or calls ahead to rent. And everyone swears by long-sleeve crewnecks that

wick moisture and can be layered under everything else. You may also want to consider adapting to the culture you're visiting—such as Africa, as Fiori does—by wearing more subdued colors, like khaki.

For the city-bound voyage, our number-one add-on is a good pair of walking shoes. It's also very cool to wear dresses all day with flip-flops or low-rise waterproof boots. Be sure to leave your umbrella home. You can get one at the hotel so you don't need to waste valuable suitcase space.

As for the car trip, if you're in the car in jeans and a lot of sweaters, you'll need a well-deserved pick-me-up, so give it to yourself. Always bring high heels for your self-esteem, not necessarily your itinerary. After all, as Lucy Sykes-Rellie says of her visits to close friends in the countryside who have children, "You're doing mommy things all day, so be a hot mom in the evening."

Going on a cruise? Life aboard ship is a lot more casual these days, unless you're going on the Crystal or Silversea lines. So Fiori underscores this more casual theme with clothes that are also lightweight: two bathing suits, shorts if it's really warm, a pair of silk slacks, a silk or chiffon top, and a wrap, because "we live in an air-conditioned world." It's easy to have things laundered on a cruise, but if you don't want to spend

INSIDER SECRET

Nothing does double duty climate-wise like a colorful quilted jacket, a perfect pashmina, and a sleek vest. The right carry-on bag takes you from plane to meeting and on to dinner.

the money, these wardrobe picks are usually lightweight enough to wash yourself.

The basics of the romantic getaway? The number-one faux pas on the road, says our FFF style squad, is that we generally don't bring anything really dressy. This is your chance. We mean lace; we mean sexy; we mean cleavage. As Barneys New York Creative Director Simon Doonan adds, "Indulge yourself in vanity on holiday with your husband (or boyfriend), and he will get to discover the cute broad you were when he met you!" Metzner adds, "Always bring something pretty to sleep in." If four-inch heels aren't your style, wear kitten heels or, like our host Rebecca does, a nice mule that can do double duty on the plane. And don't forget the Top Theory of Life—it's your upper half he'll see when he leans over that table and tells you you look gorgeous!

As for the spa vacation, our resident irreverent Doonan says take nothing but a novel. After all, this is the one trip where you're meant to do nothing at all—no shopping, no thinking, no planning what to do. And yes, our favorite spa provides tees and shorts and we bring, well, a pair of flip-flops and some clean underwear. Of course, if you want to, you can pack more than a tee or two, but do lighten your load for the spa trip.

For short hauls or weekends away, the number-one rule of the road is: Be sure to underpack! Because the trip is short, you don't want to waste any time at all packing and unpacking. James

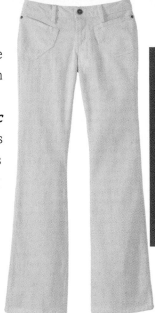

Host HINT

To avoid makeup madness, our host Rebecca Budig swears by a simple dab of lip gloss in warmer climates, where a tan is the best makeup of all. If you're not going lip-bare, we like a plain go-with-anything cranberry lipstick. And be sure to keep your hair sleek, even if it's in a ponytail (you can spritz it with water). Our host wears hers pulled back in a casual bun or clean-looking braids.

Aguiar suggests packing one pair of jeans (which you can also wear), a pair of khakis, and if you want to go out at night, a chic cashmere sweater to go with the pants. He also suggests wearing a comfortable pair of black sport shoes that blend in at night. Prada is known for them, but you can buy them at most fashionable shoe stores. Of course, if you want to pack a pair of pumps, do so.

Now our Accessories Alert. Never bring real jewelry. Instead our experts suggest packing as many of your favorite inexpensive fakes as you'd like. Think a Chanel-style charm necklace and maybe a pair of thick wooden bracelets and/or a bunch of loose bangles. A Pucci-style scarf (or one with the seasonal or more traditional pattern of your choice) will dress up a black dress. If you're tempted to bring anything with sentimental value, bring a family picture instead.

And enjoy your high-style life on the road!

the top ten

FFF GORGEOUS GETAWAYS DOS AND DON'TS

DO

Pack chiffon—it's chic, sleek, and lightweight, especially in the form of a versatile evening skirt.

Drop the droopy bag—unless you want to look saggy yourself.

Resist the ruffles and the pleats— they get crushed in your suitcase.

Take along stylish shoes—even if they're casual and comfortable.

Take along a wrap–style dress or two—as designer Diane von Furstenberg knows, it's the ultimate go-anywhere, do-anything, sexy and stylish must-pack.

DON'T

Travel in your everyday sweats or hang-around-the-house-or-neighborhood clothes—unless you want to look sloppy.

Travel in cargos—sleek trousers take you the world over.

Wear a denim jacket—opt for a stylish blazer instead.

Pack real jewelry—we say this: no expense, no worry.

Take a lot of clothes to a spa— you're there to relax, not to ponder your outfits.

CASUAL-TIES

Dear Full Frontal Fashion:

I'm a teacher at a local elementary school and to be honest with you, I dress like a dork. Right now, I'm in Starbucks wearing an old cardigan with a T-shirt that doesn't seem to match, jeans, and beat-up sneakers. Many of my friends look great, even when they're just hanging out. Where am I going wrong?

THE DORK

hardly alone so we beg you to banish the evil self-judgments! A quick style tour of some popular hot spots in our home city of New York reveals one universal American fashion truth: Not many of us take great pains to look even close to our best when we leave home. Here's what we observed: jeans with so many stains we figured they hadn't been washed in many a year; out-of-proportion outfits—think baggy barn jackets and windbreakers that cut you, dear reader, off at the thickest part of your thighs (one designer used to laughingly call this angle "90 degrees to the flab"); floor-length coats, a virtual universal casual-tie, or wardrobe blunder, because they make many of us, especially the petite among us, look like walking sausages (ouch!). And, of course, we found most of you in that beloved American mainstay—sweats that look rumpled from hours on the treadmill (keep the exercise; ax the clothes). Let it be known (and do read our Date chapter, Chapter 6) that if it's love you want, do trade up from the sweaty sweats. We're not sure he'd want to whisper a sweet hello in your fashion ear!

Needless to say, some of you don't care about fashion casual-ties—but we venture a guess that you may not know (some of us didn't) that all you need in your closet are the Top Ten Elements of Casual Style and you'll be chic, polished, and cool-looking 24/7. You'll also be ready for anything that happens to come along—the job, the love of your life, the upgrade on the plane . . . and you won't have to sacrifice the comfort and ease you love.

Now, our Full Frontal Fashion Top Ten Rules of the Casual game:

1. **QUALITY COMES FIRST.** Contrary to what may seem obvious, *quality makes a far bigger difference style-wise* when it comes to casual clothes than dressier ones. That's why author and style expert Lloyd Boston smartly suggests that we take or make the time to buy that perfect pair of jeans, that perfect twinset, that oh-so-chic leather jacket (the celebs have known this for years).

2. **FASHION COMES NEXT.** After you've acquired those perfect "basic" "signature" casual pieces, go ahead and *add lots* of more "disposable" ones—say, dime-store T-shirts or tanks, or an inexpensive knockaround leather jacket in a fun color (and as we told you in Chapter 4 on Travel, these are the wonderful things you pack—if you lose them, you won't be upset).

3. **FEMININITY FOLLOWS.** Know that nearly all fab casual pieces originated as staples of the menswear wardrobe; for this reason, we do suggest *"feminizing"* them—for example, add a soft top to a pair of pinstripe pants, or wear a flirty skirt with a muscle tee.

4. **DRESS FOR YOUR BODY TYPE.** We'll give you the full scoop in Chapter 7, but casual clothes, even more than dressier ones, can quickly become casual-ties by virtue of their fit—or lack thereof. Jeans, for instance, do not flatter every pair of hips and may not launch more than rude stares. So be sure to look in a three-way mirror and *be honest with yourself*.

5. **DRESS YOUR AGE.** It's not fashionable to say so, but many a style pro these days says, secretly, that just because we knock 'em dead in skin-tight jeans at twenty-one doesn't mean the same jeans will help us at forty-one (we still knock 'em dead of course). So stay open, *dress your best at any age* by updating your closet, and don't go lemming-like into that casual good night.

6. **FITNESS IS YOUR NUMBER-ONE ACCESSORY.** It may seem odd for us to talk about exercise in a comprehensive style book, but there is no category of fashion that benefits more from your *lifting a few weights or taking a regular walk* around the block. While the business wardrobe lets you routinely cover yourself with a jacket, the core items of casual chic—skinny jeans, say, or a fitted tee—are less forgiving.

7. **A GREAT HANDBAG IS YOUR NUMBER-TWO.** Don't leave home without it and *don't use one that's beat up*, even if you need to change bags before you go. We adore them slightly oversized and in white or fun colors, available at almost every department store or boutique.

8. **IT'S ALL IN THE MIX.** Please do read our final chapter on becoming your own stylist—and know that no category of fashion benefits from mixing and matching and pulling apart and recombining more than the casual group. That's because, unlike a suit or a dress, you're *dealing exclusively with individual items* (or, as the insiders call them, "separates"), so a pair of jeans or cool pinstripe pants, or a great white shirt, are, well, just another pair of jeans or pants or a shirt until you add a shrunken metallic

jacket and put your hair up in a messy bun; then your style becomes hot, cool, sleek, edgy, chic, and fun.

9. **TRY EVERYTHING ON.** When you visit your favorite boutique and see a great sweater that seems to scream your name, we on the FFF style squad say don't just buy it; instead, take the time to picture it as part of your closet (see Chapter 9), or *take it home and try it on* with your favorite partner piece. If it doesn't work, shop some more, or return it. As we on the FFF team have learned, a lonely piece is never casual chic.

10. **LOOK AT THE ADS; READ THE MAGS.** Stores like the Gap, for instance, likely pay a lot of money to stylists to assemble casual wardrobes for the likes of Sarah Jessica Parker. Look at these high-quality ads and *pick up ideas* that work for you. Ditto for the fashion mags.

So here goes, our own Full Frontal Fashion tour of everything you need to know to leave home when you're not working, looking *très* sophisticated and hip to boot—and never ever be a casual-tie.

THE LUXE LEATHER JACKET

Like nearly all of our Top Ten Elements of Casual Style, the leather jacket has its roots in menswear, more specifically in military styles dating to the early part of the twentieth century. Think the iconic aviator's jacket. Since then, it's become the ultimate style symbol of cool, of the heroic, even of, well, naughtiness and danger.

We strongly suggest following author and style expert Lloyd Boston's smart advice: Begin by adding a soft one- or two-button leather blazer to your closet (black is a good color choice). As Boston says, this one style alone will take you everywhere, from the office (if

you're not sure if leather is work appropriate, says Boston, simply look at your boss; if he or she is in leather, go for it; if not, skip it) to cocktails, and beyond (you may want to watch the celebs on the red carpet!).

It is key, too, says Boston, that your first jacket not only be more "classic" than other elements of the casual wardrobe, but that it be of high quality. Thus, we say, follow these three quality rules: First, ask yourself, is it soft? Next, take the scratch test. Using the back of your fingernail, "scratch" the jacket carefully; if it bounces back easily, the quality is likely good. And third, remember: Quality and longevity are not necessarily the same. Just because your jacket is buttery soft doesn't mean it will last you the rest of your life. It will, however, look amazing, as Boston says, so we say definitely dip into your bank account.

Finally, like most classic items, the leather jacket has morphed from the more traditional bomber/aviator styles (which we still adore) to trendier ones. Witness the myriad white-leather versions so popular with celebrities, and the glimmering motorcycle styles now in every color of the rainbow. Boston suggests your next purchase (if you can afford two) be something in brown—we love a slightly cropped and fitted jacket style that will, again, take you to work, to post-work events, on a date, and possibly even to a black-tie optional affair.

Speaking of which, if the celebrities are any indication, dressier occasions can be ideal for leather. The late Geoffrey Beene knew this all too well with his ultra-chic little shrunken black-leather toppers that went into evening (with sleek pants or even a jumpsuit) in a flash. And, as Boston notes, celebrities have long understood one extraordinary benefit of the leather jacket—notably, that it reflects the light back onto your own gorgeous face. Very little, including rhinestone earrings, can match this asset.

And remember, to make a leather jacket edgy, just follow the FFF rule and pair this more masculine, severe, or hard-edged item with a softer and more feminine one. So, like the celebs, you can wear your leather blazer with a flirty chiffon sparkle skirt and a lacy white cami, or a pair of slimming dark-wash jeans, a colorful and sexy top, and great pair of sexy shoes or ankle boots.

INSIDER SECRET

Celebrities have long known the power of the leather jacket, says author and style expert Lloyd Boston. This casual chic essential rivals even glittery earrings when it comes to reflecting light and thus brightening up your entire face.

Can you blunder with leather? Not really, but we do advise that you take good care of it by finding the best leather cleaner in your area.

THE GREAT WHITE SHIRT

As Valerie Steele, the director and chief curator of the Museum at the Fashion Institute of Technology in New York, notes, the white shirt is another menswear symbol with a long and revered style history: It has been considered the anchor of a man's wardrobe and, more important, has long been thought of as a status symbol (think "white collar" versus "blue collar"). That ranking derives from the fact that it was the supremely wealthy who could afford to send their white shirts out to be laundered, sometimes over long distances, just to achieve the right press and polish.

Well, plenty has changed, but we on the Full Frontal style team still say, yes, do make sure you have a great white shirt (or two, or even more) in your closet. As Boston says, "It's a canvas you can build on." Boston insists that you have a "staple" shirt, and that it be a more traditional, tailored button-down style— but that doesn't mean it has to be boring! Unlike in earlier decades (even the 1980s), these days your "essential" white shirt can be fitted, and have interesting if not exotic buttons (Lloyd suggests mother-of-pearl; we've also seen great shirts with covered buttons). It can be fashioned from head-turning fabric (Boston loves a chunkier cotton piqué, but feel free to choose anything from eyelet—we love this—to silk to a range of choices with a bit of stretch to them). He also strongly suggests that your staple shirt have darts (and we couldn't agree more!). Nothing makes you look more feminine, ladylike, and sleek.

Needless to say, like most of our essential casual elements, the white shirt has morphed from traditional to tweaks-on-traditional to just about anything you can think of fashion-wise. So for your number-two white shirt, we say go for it—and know that the more fashion your shirt

has, the more likely it can double as a jacket, or at least stand alone, sometimes as your outfit's show-stopper. Some fashionable styles we love: double collars, wraparounds, ruffles or tuxedo detailing, gathering at the mid-section (it always makes us look slimmer), corseting up the side, and Edwardian detailing.

As for mixing that white shirt up, Boston recommends pairing it as a stand-alone with a simple pencil skirt or pair of chic stovepipe or cigarette pants. Wear the pants with boots, whether you live in L.A., N.Y., or in between, and whether it's summer or winter. If you want to buy a cutting-edge fabric, we love traditional ones like poplin combined with some stretch or an interesting detail. If you wear earrings, invest in a decent pair of gold or silver drops. The white and the bright will make your face pop. Anything you pair with a great white shirt (as long as it's clean and well-pressed) will be raised to another level. It is truly cool and stylish.

Dearest "Dork"—this is your answer! Grab your purse and get those shopping feet moving! And don't let your shirt become a casual-tie by letting it yellow (notably by leaving it in a dry-cleaning bag; see Chapter 9 on Editing Your Closet).

THE PERFECT SWEATER SET

The perfect sweater set took center stage—and was viewed as very edgy, mind you—back in the 1920s with Chanel; it then skyrocketed to more glory (with lots of glamour) in the 1950s with a bevy of hourglass-shaped movie stars (sometimes tagged "sweater girls") who relied on it to convey that unmistakable allure of sportiness, sexiness, glamour, and politesse. Lately, there's been a switch back—what seemed edgy back then (the idea that women could wear something as sporty as a sweater actually broke new fashion ground, as the Fashion Institute's Valerie Steele knows all too well) has now taken on the appeal of your mom's old head scarf.

So what to do? Well, our FFF pro Lloyd Boston suggests following the same tack that we've traveled for our other Top Ten Elements of Casual Style: Make sure you invest in a twinset that is high quality, such as one in cashmere. It is timeless,

traditional, and conveys quality. Buy a set that is multiple-ply ("ply" refers to the number of strands twisted together to form the yarn) to prevent it from pilling. Cashmere is sold by weight, so although a lower-ply sweater will be cheaper, it may not be sturdy enough to guarantee a long shelf life. Rather than opting for a single ply, if you can't afford 100 percent cashmere, choose a blend of cashmere (at least 20 percent) with something soft, lightweight, and luxurious like silk.

And if you want to give a more classic sweater set an edge (after all, you're not your mom) do it by pairing it with "amazing edgy bottoms," as Boston says. Lloyd suggests these au courant mixes: a skirt that's a little higher in the waist and accessorized with a great knee-boot; or even a wonderful avant-garde skirt by a cutting-edge designer (think frayed hemlines), accessorized with chunky necklaces.

As for that second choice, a non-staple sweater set or sets that you can actually buy in bulk, well, the stores are chock full of them—trimmed in ruffles, metallic, lace, fur, and sequins; embroidered, tie-dyed, and speckled with punchy patterns on the side; with jeweled buttons, one big button, no buttons, and ribbon closures; belted and wrapped; with three-quarter sleeves and short sleeves; shrunken, cropped, and extra-long; fashioned from a thick ivory fisherman's style cableknit and super-fine multihued twisted yarn.

Our favorite sweater-set tactic is to pull it apart—why not buy two colors to begin with or a long cardigan over a shorter shell?—and then mix it up some more. The day we photographed designer Shoshanna Lonstein Gruss in her lively showroom for an episode of *Full Frontal Fashion's Top Ten*, she was selling terrific sets in mix-and-match summer brights (think orange and turquoise) with a choice of silver or gold metallic trim on the shell and metallic buttons on the cardigan. We also love mixing necklines in unexpected ways, say a V-neck with a crew, or a boatneck layered over a camisole-style knit shell. Also try a lace-trimmed cardigan with three-quarter sleeves over a dress in a contrasting color; a shrunken short-sleeved version with dressy gold buttons over shorts; and another FFF top pick—a casual cardigan over a dressier metallic bustier.

Your only casual-tie, says celebrity stylist James Aguiar, is owning the finest cashmere (or even the less than finest) and not taking care of it. (We urge you to read Chapter 9. Hint, hint: You do not want to put your cardigans on wire hangers!)

CHIC JEANS

Jeans, the garment that is widely considered the number one addition to world style began, as Valerie Steele notes, as part of an ordinary man's work wardrobe. In the 1940s and then again in the 1960s, they took on an association with youth and with rebellion (often involving left-wing politics). These days, they are still a symbol of youth and, most importantly, as Steele continues to explain, of authenticity. There's nothing phony about jeans! Isn't that why we love them so much?

But unlike our other great symbols of casual style, jeans are very trend-sensitive, so buying one "classic" or traditional pair and then backing it up with the less-pricey fun stuff won't work. The best way to buy chic jeans is to buy whatever is cool, is "in," is hip. According to Boston, that means investing in a truly high-quality pair (of whatever you love), even if that means taking your time—and a close friend or boyfriend with you whom you trust to tell you the fashion truth when you shop with them. A number of us on the FFF style team happen to like black jeans. As both Boston and Steele note, contrary to the myth that jeans are comfortable, they are in fact

one of the most unforgiving items of clothing you can own—which is another reason to shop carefully and take your time. And don't assume jeans are for everyone—if you look better in a pair of flat-front trousers or a pinstripe or lean-gauge cord, go for it.

A few more FFF *chic-jeans rules*: Do spend more money on this one great pair if you have to; do buy a dark wash first; don't shop by label and do shop by fit. Boot cuts flatter lots of body types; cropped do not (especially if you're petite); back pocket flaps do a bigger butt make; and a fit that is loose on the bottom will balance bigger hips on the upper body; you may also want to watch fabrics that are too stretchy (for more insider secrets, be sure to see Chapter 7 on remaining Fit & Flawless). Boston also recommends letting your jeans age and wear in naturally—a look he considers far more chic than anything fake and factory-worn.

Finally, for your next pair (or pairs) of jeans, go for styling in

another fabric—think velvet (bottoms only; too much velvet can weigh you down) or pinstripes or cotton; and do mix the pieces up wisely—on the red carpet (and in fashion magazines), nothing is more chic and classic than jeans and a great Chanel or Chanel-style jacket.

We hate to repeat ourselves, but one casual-tie you don't want to make is this: If the jeans don't fit, don't wear them. We see too many Don'ts as it is!

WHEN YOU NEED MORE THAN CARGOS

Cargos are based on military styles, but we on the FFF style team want something edgier—and there has never been a better time to shop for it. Prompted by Boston, we suggest a pair of stovepipe pants or a great pair of linen ones (Boston says he loves nothing more than a quality pair when its wrinkles form naturally); gray flannels or even cotton canvas with subtle (and slimming) pinstripes would also work for us.

You can also opt for a pair in a traditional fabric that has edgy styling—for instance, gray wool flares; or in a nighttime fabric that becomes edgy during the day—like a seasonless cotton sateen, or black with a subtle tuxedo stripe.

Today, it's all about how you wear your trousers—say, maybe a little bit slouchy, with a contrasting ribbon or scarf belt and a sexier lace cami to balance the masculinity of trousers with the femininity of the belt and the top. You can also balance masculine with feminine with lots of bracelets or a great pair of dressy flats (think Marc Jacobs), or by opting for trousers in more feminine white, with a flirty top in a floral print.

Remember that it's slimming to wear the darker color on the bottom. Not long ago, in a major bookstore, we spotted Annie Herz, the clerk we mentioned earlier who caught our eye because she had figured out the impossible: how to be cool in wine-colored trousers. How'd she do it? In a sleek top, wearing great glasses. She stood out from the crowd and looked chic and hip and put together to boot.

Finally, an **FFF Wardrobe Warning** for casual-tie prevention: If you are eyeing a style that is potentially unforgiving and/or unflatter-ing on many body types—such as riding styles or cropped pants—look in a three-way mirror first. And don't forget: Most people see more of your back than your front.

THE PERFECT TEE

Originally, the T-shirt was, of course, men's underwear. According to the Fashion Institute's Steele, it started to inch its way into our clos-ets around the 1920s, and by the 1970s it had morphed into the outerwear we think of today. These days, of course, the tee morphs nonstop—we now have tees in every color of the rainbow, in every neckline, with every sleeve style, in loads of fabrics. You can opt for a tight fit and seaming; or, as we did for one of our choice pho-tos, ribbing with a higher armhole, in a favorite shade of light blue.

What Valerie Steele says about jeans also applies to tees: What looks simple and striking really requires legwork. If you want to truly go out in tee style, it may take you a while to find the perfect one. Be sure to think about what you'll be wearing it with and how those other items will look with the neckline, the sleeve length, the armhole fit, and the color. If it does fit to a T, buy more than one—and do not gripe about price. A good tee,

whether under your business suit, with a great satin evening skirt, a more voluminous and casual skirt, or even a sleek mini, or by itself, is a wardrobe gem. (Our faves have come from the great Japanese designers like Rei Kawakubo of Comme des Garçons).

After your good tee(s), we don't mind your buying stacks of them from your nearby drugstore or choice low-cost retailer, but chic most of these tees are not. They are, purely and simply, throwaway fashion.

THE SLEEK TOPPER

Our topper of choice is the trench coat, which (guess what?) began as a military style for men (think trench warfare or in the trenches) and later became the mysterious wardrobe staple of spies. It really is a raincoat and, for all its style variations in recent years, it is a fully functional must-have. We repeat: an absolute must-have.

If you can afford it, get the very best trench you can find, make sure it is well-lined, has zippers that work, and has a cloth belt (the trench is meant to be tied, not buckled). It must protect you against the elements. Any neutral shade is always a good choice. Be sure, too, that it is a figure-flattering three-quarter length; long raincoats, as we noted earlier, are a casual-tie.

After you have a classic safely in your closet, have fun buying a trendier one—think animal prints, leather, cotton florals, brocade, satin, tweed, camel hair; shorter and boxier, with toggle closures or covered buttons. (Note: Designers have sent

more than a few trench coat dresses down the runway that have very little, if anything, underneath. No one ever said they weren't versatile!)

In addition to the trench, we also nominate the anorak (also derived from men's military uniforms). One of the iconic ones is designed by Prada—in our walk along Park Avenue you couldn't miss them—always in black with the perfect lightweight fabric, pockets, length, and chic quotient. We love parkas or anoraks in fun colors, too.

THE BEST TURTLENECK

Though on Katharine Hepburn it was quite glamorous, these days, some of our pros admit, the basic turtleneck is somewhat less popular than it used to be (in its place is the creative T-neck—think collars that are slit, draped, ribbed, sequined; a body that is ribbed in so many innovative and contrasting ways we've literally lost fashion count). We do, however, happen to love the simple, soft, close-to-the-body turtlenecks fashioned from silky second-skin fabrics.

And remember: A good turtleneck will take you from day to night, even to black-tie optional dinners—especially one that is sleeveless and fashioned from the finest cashmere. Our favorite outfit is a great turtleneck with a sexy, nearly see-through evening skirt.

A FFF Wardrobe Warning: On a date, a turtleneck may not be your mate. An open neckline signals that you, too, are open, friendly, and available.

FFF WARDROBE WARNING

On a date, a turtleneck may not be your mate. An open neckline signals that you, too, are open, friendly, and available.

THE PERFECT LOAFER

Our team has found that some of you don't really like loafers; after all, they don't give you that sexy leg-up that comes with a pair of heels. Still, among the fashion cognoscenti, nothing is more sophisticated than the right pair of driving shoes (the icon for this is Tod's) or a pair of loafers in a metallic color (especially when worn with white jeans; see Chapter 4). We also strongly suggest Belgian loafers for their more feminine look.

Then, of course, you can splurge on a simple pair of fun flats or slip-ons—many of them nowadays come in loafer-like styling, in great colors and often in suede, which we love. Ditto for some updated moccasins and ballerina flats.

THE SOPHISTICATED SCARF

Scarves began as a "useful thing" that soldiers wore around their necks during battle. Often, the scarf doubled as a tourniquet. By the late seventeenth century, the scarf began to show up as a fashion—this time for show; men also wore it as a cravat. As for the infamous patterned silk quadrangle, well, that likely became popular with women much later in the twentieth century, says Valerie Steele.

While your mom's patterned scarves—think Hermès—carried a lot of status, the cutting edge today isn't so much the pattern (although we love the horsey imprimatur)—it's where on your body you wear it, and whether or not you know how to tie it. We love a bright shot of color (polka dots are fine) at the neck with a great, colorful trench coat. A big, patterned scarf (think Pucci) can make a great belt, especially when your trousers are baggy and you want to draw the eye to your waistline for an hourglass look. You can also use it as an on-site addition to an empire waist dress; obi-style, with a pair of satin jeans; around the handle of a chic slouchy bag; or, mimicking celebs, a great square on your head.

As for knowing how to tie it, as *Harper's Bazaar's* executive fashion and beauty editor Avril Graham told us in Chapter 2, if you don't know how to tie it, don't wear it. This is a casual-tie. She also pointed out that stores like Hermès provide an instruction card. Please do ask for one.

10

the top ten
FFF CASUAL AND CASUAL-TIES DOS AND DON'TS

DO

Buy yourself a superb leather jacket—the right one is the celeb must-have and a day-to-evening staple.

Feminize your more masculine clothes—if it's menswear-inspired, pair it with something ladylike.

Make a classic sweater set edgy—by pairing it with edgy bottoms.

Invest in a great pair of jeans—when it comes to jeans, fit equals fab.

Dress for your body type—be sure to look in a three–way mirror, take an honest buddy shopping with you, and read Chapter 7.

DON'T

Wear a boring turtleneck—that is, if you want to be stylish.

Wear a scarf if you can't tie it—you'll be a casual-tie for sure.

Wear a white shirt that's yellow—not only will the shirt be off-color, you will be, too.

Buy cashmere that is too loosely knit—it may fall apart, and your outfit will, too.

Buy prewashed jeans—if they're not naturally worn in, they're not chic.

DATE
DRESSING

Dear Full Frontal Fashion:

I've never liked dating. That's probably why I've put it off for so long.

My friends keep telling me to use the Internet and I just keep ignor-

ing them—until now. I turn thirty on Monday and I feel like the clock

is ticking, so I finally took the plunge. I have my first date tomorrow,

but instead of feeling excited I'm sitting here stressing about what to

wear. Is there a "date wardrobe" I need to buy for this? I just don't

feel right in what I have in my closet. Can you advise me—quickly?

TO BUY OR NOT TO BUY

Dear "To Buy or Not to Buy," we on the Full Frontal Fashion style squad will begin with our number-one date-dressing rule: Nothing is more important when you step out looking for love than feeling good in your clothes. It's not about the money (if you just bought a great fringed Chanel-style jacket and it feels too trendy, don't wear it on a date!). If you own a vintage blouse that cost you five dollars and you feel like a million bucks in it, that's the topper for you—with a bottom you love just as much.

Now to the nitty gritty: Very few stores—or even designers, for that matter—design with "dating" in mind. It's not a category like casual, evening wear, or business. It's no secret that many of us (including more than a few on our own Full Frontal team) are, as we speak, shopping for date clothes. And we say this to the world of high fashion: With this guide, we anoint Date Dressing as a full-fledged wardrobe category.

So what's the poor, time-starved dater to do? Our advice is, follow our **Top Ten rules (and ten bonus ones!) for finding love in fashion:**

1. **DON'T WEAR TOO MANY TRENDS.** Nothing turns a man off more than this.

2. **DON'T WEAR TOO MUCH MAKEUP.** Ditto above.

3. **MEN LOVE COLOR.** We on the FFF squad can't give you a scientific survey but the mad daters among us (and that includes many a magazine writer who has researched the subject thoroughly) has found that the male is entranced by a *colorful pivot*.

4. **FIT IS FAB.** Forget New Year's resolutions. There is no better time to pump a little iron or take a daily walk than now.

5. **DRESS FOR YOURSELF.** The average guy can't tell if you are in a five-thousand-dollar Chanel or a two-dollar eBay so don't bother dressing for him (at least early on). Dress for yourself and, more importantly, *be yourself!* If your Fashion Personality is Classic, be Classic; if it's more Fashion Forward, stay forward. Nothing turns a guy off more than finding out six months down the line that the frilly boob-revealing numbers he couldn't take his eyes off hid a true sweatsuit-o-holic.

6. **MAKE THE MOST OF WHAT YOU'VE GOT.** As Jeffrey Kalinsky,

the style brains behind Jeffrey, one of New York City's best known designer stores (and a choice haven for celebs, assorted heiresses, and down-to-earth glam folks like us) says, begin by *identifying your assets*; then decide how you want to approach these assets. If you have a big bust, for instance, decide if you want to show it off or not, then dress accordingly. And know that either decision is fine.

7. **FEEL GOOD—BUT DON'T STOP THERE.** As Kalinsky advises his clients, "look in the mirror and say, 'Do I feel sassy?' If you *feel sassy*, you're dressed right for a date."

8. **IT'S ALL IN THE UNDERWEAR.** As Betsey Johnson told one of us in a magazine interview a while back, a great trick if you want to feel sexy on a date is simply this: Don't wear underwear. To be reasonable, *we suggest a thong*. It's not so much the outer clothes that help you feel sexy; it's what you've got going on underneath. Moreover, you won't be showing those panty lines in jeans.

9. **GET HELP IF YOU NEED IT.** We recently spotted Andrea Sorenson, twenty-eight, at Intermix, one of our favorite boutiques and a date-dressing haven in New York (especially for those last-minute style decisions). Andrea came in looking for a pick-me-up for an Internet date that very night. She also arrived, if we may be so bold, looking in need of a Cinderella lift. Well, after the Intermix staff helped her, we literally couldn't take our eyes off the dazzling transformation: Sorenson in a little light-blue pleated skirt (flirty yet classy), a light-blue sweater with a tasteful, shoulder-revealing neckline, opaque hose and a great pair of low pointy-toed shoes with a sling back. And we want you to know, it was the *wonderful sales staff* that helped her address her immediate needs—so don't be afraid to get up from your computer (you can e-mail those future dates later) and head over to your best boutique for that easy mood boost.

10. **FORGET TURTLENECKS.** As we noted, your neck is the one body part that lets men know you are open, available, and welcoming—think of it as *message central* for love on dates one through ten—so don't cover it up.

11. **SOFT SELLS.** Men love soft fabrics—we say nothing beats *angora*.

12. **MEN LOVE SKIRTS.** We're not saying you have to; we're just reporting what we've found.

13. **SACK THE SLUTTINESS.** If you want to bed him on date one, slutty might work (it also might intimidate him), but if it's love you're after, *dress in style*. You'll feel better about yourself and he'll feel better about you (or at least about taking you home to Mom).

14. **GO FEMININE—OR EVEN GIRLY.** We're not saying drop your Fashion Personality, we're simply advising you to *add a touch or two of the big fem*. One of our buddies who attracts men (decent ones!) like flies to a swatter ascribes her success to: 1) friendliness (in a neutral way); and 2) Dressing somewhat girlishly. This can be as easy as a soft color—like the light blue worn by our budding Cinderella in number 9 above—or a fabric like angora.

15. **DON'T DRESS FOR THE ACADEMY AWARDS.** "You don't want to overwhelm him and have it be all about fashion," says Boardman. "You want to *dress mysteriously* and be sexy without being in-your-face." Remember, though: Dressier than the man is better than more casual.

16. **NO BAGGY CLOTHES OR "HIDING OUT."** As Kalinsky says only half-jokingly, "You don't want to feel too comfortable in your own skin—that means you're not trying!"

17. **DON'T REPEAT YOURSELF FOR THE FIRST MONTH.** As the daters on our expert team can tell you, men like *"change"* (so do we, although we like the word "freshness"!). "Keep reinventing yourself," urges Kalinsky.

18. **TALK TO YOUR MALE FRIENDS.** That way you'll find out how simple date-dressing really is. Not long ago, one of our closest male pals told one style-stumped dater among us that she looked "amazing" in the fitted white shirt she had on that day (for a meditation at a local center). Just the look in

his eye told us it was a date winner. So if there's a guy whose date taste you trust, ask him for a bit of input.

19. **DON'T FORGET YOUR FACE.** It's your greatest asset and it's where his eyes will wander for most of your date (at least if you're in a restaurant or café). *Go for a healthy look.* And don't forget a touch of natural-looking gloss and blush. Avoid foundation (as Kalinsky says, "Unless you absolutely need it, foundation should be saved for stage makeup") and be sure to keep the look dewy (gloss, crème blush, a thin layer of tinted moisturizer or sunscreen). And remember: Matte will not a mate attract.

20. **FINALLY, TREAT A DATE LIKE A SPECIAL OCCASION.** If you can't get up the steam to dress for your date, we strongly urge you to treat it as a special occasion—and then, as Boardman says, it will become one. Your best bet? Take an hour and go in for a blow-dry or *treat yourself to a casual up-do.* You, the intrepid dater, deserve it.

THE FIRST DATE

This is the date to accentuate what you've got (and to read our next chapter, Fit & Flawless). And you want to choose a date locale with a wide style vortex—most restaurants fit that bill these days. And you want to look shapely (men are very shape-driven), but you don't want to come-hither him like Samantha in *Sex and the City. Sex and the City* was not reality TV, especially when it comes to date-dressing. The first date is the leave-something-to-his-imagination date.

So, if you've got great legs, for example, and you're going to a restaurant with an anything-goes dress code, we advise you to show off those gams with a great skirt, perhaps with a small front or side slit (it's too soon for sky-high on the

thigh); a bare leg instead of hose is great if you can manage it (especially in warm weather) and a great pair of mid-height heels (we love mules). As Kalinsky advises his clients, always wear heels on dates (unless you're a basketball star), but we say leave the stilettos to his imagination for now. Finally, on date one, if you're wearing one sexy item (say a slit skirt), balance it with another that is a little more sedate, perhaps a simple nicely fitted blouse or sweater rather than a top that is so sexy he can't concentrate on his meal. That way you'll be cool—and nothing, mind you, nothing, is more intriguing to him than cool.

FFF WARDROBE WARNING

Don't dress for sex—or he could just be your ex. Do, however, wear a thong. As Jeffrey Kalinsky, owner of the ultra-chic Jeffrey designer stores, says, it's a *must* from date one to zap panty lines.

You may also want to designate a First Date outfit so you don't have to think about it—or even worry about it. Susan Zelnick is a close buddy of ours who has fifteen years of dating experience (she is now engaged). She remembers nearly every piece of stylish clothing she has ever bought for each date, in part because she has always included dating among the situations she regularly shops for—always at the start of each season. What she's learned, she says, is that you should update your date wardrobe and zero in on clothes that you can wear in other situations, too. Zelnick also knows that she likes to stop home after work to change for dates (she says freshening up is half the "battle").

Zelnick's tried-and-true designated First Date outfit? A pair of her favorite Theory pants (we love this label for trousers) and a simple, fitted cableknit crewneck. It works every time, she says. For a publicist for a well-known designer, it's a business suit with a comfortable fit; right before the date, however, she changes into tighter pants. Another trusty style team expert, *Paper*'s Boardman, suggests the prefect black Audrey Hepburn–style sheath dress because it flatters all figures. "And it doesn't have to be boring," he adds, "as long as you balance it with a bag, jewelry, and sexy shoes. The key is, you don't have to worry about it." We also just adore the little light-blue outfit that our buddy Andrea Sorenson wore on her Internet first date (see rule number 9, page 91). It's simple, feminine, classy, sexy, flattering—and a boost for her (and him)—and us, too.

You can only go wrong, say our pros, by being too provocative. Ladylike does a first date make.

THE BLIND DATE

We hate to say it, but the please factor comes in here. If we have a great conversation with him on the phone (or by e-mail) and we're excited, we tend to raid the closet and even shop for something new. If we feel like we want to kiss him off but we've told ourselves, "you never know," we might just experience a downturn in wardrobe enthusiasm. That's why our trusty buddy Zelnick says never—never—talk to him on the phone for more than fifteen minutes! And if you don't like him after five, cancel, dear stylish dresser, cancel.

Our Blind Date dressing rule is this: Notch it up one step from First Date dressing where the two of you have already met in some way because, as Kalinsky explains, you only get one chance to make a first impression—and first impressions count. Our advice is, especially if you're dating up a storm (as some of us are), set aside one Blind Date outfit you can rely on. And, as Boardman says, your goal is to show off your shape without being in-your-face sexy.

Our most reliable options: If you're coming from work, a designated Date Suit is ideal, especially a stylish one with an hourglass shape (this is not your corporate pantsuit date!); wear it with a camisole on a date day, or wear the jacket with nothing underneath, along with a thin necklace with interesting charms, or an eye-catching designerly piece (to draw his eye up) and an antique charm bracelet or, if you're feeling more avant-garde, clear Lucite bangles—we adore them. Know that if you like him, you can always send a signal by removing the jacket (as long as you've got that cami on). Another favorite option: the wrap dress in a fun print or color—we like black-and-white or figure-flattering stripes.

And remember Boardman's advice: never take chances on a blind date. If you want to try something different with your hair, wait 'til a later date. By the fifth, he'll know what you look like anyway. And make sure you can walk in your shoes. As Zelnick says, "Guys love to walk—and meanwhile, you're *dying*."

Can you blunder on a blind date? Yep—by being blind to the possibilities. He may just fall for you, wardrobe and all. And make sure you don't look like you spent the whole day getting date-dressed. ***Desperate Date Dressing is a no-no of major proportions.***

THE THIRD DATE

The Third Date is, as one dating member of our FFF team put it, "the make or break date." So you're notching it up again—this is the Dress Date for sure. And we don't mean a black sheath. The perfect dress is cool and sexy in a feminine way—think sultry and soft. Classic flowy Chloé is ideal; so is anything bohemian—a great filmy top that shows skin by way of its design, and a soft, flirty skirt.

A few other possibilities: If you have the body for it, Boardman suggests going for a drop-dead knit—a fun Missoni print is the style icon here. You can also go "ingenue sexy" by sporting a cute, vintage-like dress (best done by designer Marc Jacobs) and worn in top-tier style by celeb icon Kirsten Dunst. As Boardman says, it's revealing in a young and fresh way.

As for accessories, this is time to get out a sassy pair of kitten heels, says Kalinsky, especially if you've worn a different style on dates one and two. You may also want to consider investing in a pair of high-quality hose that match your skin tone—twenty dollars or more a pair may seem like highway robbery, but it's worth it to feel like you'll knock your date off his seat (and you'll also look amazing at a wedding or cocktail party or just about any upcoming RSVP event).

Can you goof? Yes—by being overdone. Remember: Too dressy is too desperate.

MEET THE PARENTS

OK, fashion stars, this is a great opportunity to wear clothes that say nothing more than that you have good taste and, as Boardman says, that "you're a pillar of the community." This is the classic suit date or the expensive-sweater-and-pretty-skirt date. Kalinsky specifically recommends a sweater set and pencil skirt—if you have the body for that latter; if not, another skirt is fine These are not, however, the everyday send-no-signal clothes you wear to a rehearsal dinner (see Chapter 3); after all, he hasn't quite gotten down on one knee yet—so do shop if you need to.

First, a few rules we've stumbled on: 1) Don't outdo Mom by a mile—you'll only look like you're so high maintenance you'll wipe out the family fortune. 2) Don't dress to please the parents, either; as Boardman wisely advises, you'll never win. 3) You only have one chance to make a good impression and, as Boardman notes, too, they'll never forget it if you dress like a hooker.

If your choice is a suit (and it's our number-one pick), simply opt for a versatile style that is a hip, modern, even whimsical take on a classic like Chanel. It can be in a color or interesting tweed; you can also wear it with an ironic attitude. This is the moment for delicate drop earrings (we love gold circles); if the accessories are not delicate, be sure they are classy and well-matched. If it's the sweater and skirt you've opted for, Kalinsky recommends any shoe or boot, pearls and/or diamond studs, and pretty makeup. "Again, I'd have my sexy lingerie on underneath," he advises, "because you never know—there's nothing like fooling around in the house where you grew up."

Finally, if it's more casual—our buddy Zelnick was invited onto her now fiancé's parents' boat—don't be afraid to ask for wardrobe input. Urban girl that she is, the admittedly nervous Zelnick needed a few dates to learn the ins and outs of water-worthy shoe-wear.

THE BIG NIGHT OUT

This is your chance to pull out the stops; to treat your date as a special occasion (if you haven't so far). This is the Sexy Dress Date (and we don't mean a cocktail number). We love anything with spaghetti straps. Kalinsky also likes a flip dress (think Dolce & Gabbana, among others). "No bells and whistles," Kalinsky says emphatically. "It's all about the cut."

Kalinsky also says this is your moment to pull out the jewelry stops—with real diamonds, dear readers. "Let him know from the beginning that you like beautiful jewelry," he says.

THE AT-YOUR-PLACE (FOR THE FIRST TIME) DATE

You can go two ways on this date: comfy (make-him-feel-at-home) or seductive. Nearly every member of our FFF style team voted for the first option. As Boardman suggests, this is when you want to curb your enthusiasm for overwhelming him. Instead, switch it down and be yourself (or at least look that way)—wear a smart-looking shrunken polo shirt and a great pair of jeans (we adore dark-wash boot-cuts) and a pair of sexy slip-ons. The message you want to send is, "I'm comfortable and at home so you can be, too." This will help both of you relax and have fun. And, as Zelnick adds, you don't want to swelter in a sweater if you're cooking dinner or worry about splattering on your Missoni. (Some free date advice: You don't want to be so busy marinating that he's busy in another room stewing; make something ahead of time. Why date-dress if you're not on view?)

You also want to make a concerted effort to put on the perfect pair of earrings (after all, you won't have a bag or dressy shoes). We say, wear whatever you love, even if they're fancy chandeliers.

More free date advice: As Kalinsky says, if he does stay over, absolutely *no* baggy sweats or shapeless robe the next morning. Plan ahead: Get up earlier than he does and slip into your "notice-me" clothes from the gym—a real cute and sexy ribbed tank top or two is ideal (Kalinsky says spare the bra if you can) and a casual bottom that fits perfectly (something patterned after Juicy Couture is fine). Then you can "get him out of the house to give yourself time to unwind and get ready for the day."

THE AT-HIS-PLACE (FOR THE FIRST TIME) DATE

The rule here is, look sexy but don't telegraph assumptions—about the relationship or, worse, about staying over (unless he's specifically asked you to). So we say this is the perfect time for a mix of messages—casual (to help him feel at ease) and less so (to be seductive). We suggest a pencil skirt (any skirt that's flattering, actually) and a tank top. If a tank is too bare or too tight, go with a T-shirt in a soft fabric or with an interesting decorative detail such as a ribbon tie or wrap front. One of our FFF full-time daters also wants us to suggest a pair of pants and a camisole (it's her fave).

But remember, as all of our team pros noted, you want to wear clothes that you can easily slip in and out of (just in case)—and that you can go home in the next day. As one famous designer reportedly noted, you don't want to be walking home at breakfast time in a pouf dress.

Your best accessory? A sleek handbag (a Tod's, or a colorful tote would be great) that is a bit oversized and can hold a toothbrush, a change of underwear, your makeup, and perhaps a hairbrush. But as Kalinsky warns, do not bring an authentic overnight bag. "Don't ever make him think you're in a comfortable place," he says.

THE LAST DATE

If you know this is your last date and you're doing the dumping, we say don't don your drop-dead frocks just to rub his nose in it. On the other hand, if you suspect he's breaking up with you (and you're actually showing up for the "kill"—let's talk about this later) you may want to look attractive enough that he's going to miss you. Then again, as one of our style team daters notes, dress hot and he may give you another shot. In any case, as Zelnick advises, you never want to look like you've been crying.

When you're the dumper, we suggest the sexy librarian look—or a stylish approximation. Go for clean and relatively buttoned up—think a man-tailored shirt that really is man-tailored (Brooks Brothers, or, for more oomph, go with Thomas Pink) and any pair of pants will do (this is not your skirt date). You can also defy the turtleneck rule and go with simple monotone dressing—the turtleneck on top and black trousers on the bottom. If you think it's you who's getting the heave-ho, switch up to a nicer, more fitted pair of pants (or even a skirt) and a great fitted top of your choice. This is also a great moment for a V-neck.

Where can you go wrong? Well, if Kalinsky is right, by finding yourself in this face-to-face position in the first place. If there's breaking up to do, he says, spare yourself and do it over the phone.

THE RUN-INTO-YOUR-EX DATE

As *Glamour*'s executive fashion editor-at-large Suze Yalof Schwartz says (in Chapter 4) on the importance of *always* looking good: *Dress as if you might run into your ex.* Which is a lot like dressing for your high school reunion—you want to telegraph the message that life couldn't be better without him.

To do that, follow our surefire rule for leaving home in style (even if you work there and run around in your pj's and food-stained sweats). Slip into a V-neck sweater—if it's cashmere, the higher the ply, the more prosperous you will look—and a great pair of pants. Our dating buddy Zelnick did this (she buys her Theory pants in a wide range of colors for occasions just like this) and guess what? She ran right into her ex, they sat on a bench in the park, and, well, they did go around one more time.

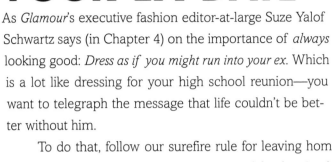

THE SPORTS DATE

The operative fashion words here are "cute, cute, cute." So if you're heading to a football game, wear a cute shrunken football jersey, says Boardman, and a pair of nice-fitting jeans or cute shorts. If it's tennis and you're playing with him, go for a cute little tennis skirt (patterns and colors are just fine) and a great shrunken polo (if you've already worn one by Lacoste at your place, try a Ralph Lauren). Again, we love colors!

And give yourself space for mistakes. Zelnick sweltered in too-heavy clothes at her first-date baseball game; next time, she knew to lighten up. As for sports date boo-boos, well, our team says forget the hair tucked under the backward baseball cap. Let's just say it's a guy thing. Tacky, tacky, tacky.

10

the top ten

FFF DATE DRESSING DOS AND DON'TS

DO

Have a designated date outfit (or two or three)—ready, set, go out and get 'em!

Accentuate your assets—you've got them, so use them.

Wear natural-looking makeup—dating and face paint don't mix.

Get help if you need it—especially from date-friendly boutiques.

Kick it up for the blind date—you only get one chance at a first impression.

DON'T

Be provocative on the first date—unless you want to go home with him that night.

Be too dressy—dressy can look desperate.

Look like you spent all day getting ready—this is the mating call of the desperate dater.

Wear flats—unless you're on a boat or are a basketball star.

Pack a real overnight bag your first time at his place—unless he's personally asked you in advance to stay over.

FLAWLESS

Dear Full Frontal Fashion:

I love tops with plunging necklines but whenever I wear them I look a little brazen because I have such large breasts. My smaller-chested friends don't have that problem! What can I do?

PLUNGING

Dear "Plunging" nothing is more important in the wardrobe department than assessing your assets (and large breasts can be one) and finessing (or camouflaging) your "flaws." Learn to master the confidence game (see Chapter 10) generally by choosing stylish clothes in which you feel really good.

So, here, our *Top Ten Rules for feeling good about what you've got:*

1. **WEIGHT NOT, WANT NOT.** If you're waiting to shed those extra pounds before you take the next step in your fashion life, we say don't! Nothing is more passé than playing the weighting game.

2. **BE SIZE WISE.** As the *Wall Street Journal*'s senior special writer Teri Agins wisely explains, many fashion companies make clothes in universal sizes that they estimate will fit a wide range of body types—that doesn't mean their size ten is your size ten. Some of us are a two one day and a ten the next, so relax and pay your size no mind. Here's an insider secret: More than a few top celebrity stylists clip the sizes out of clothes before they show them to their body-obsessed clients—some even go so far as to sew in labels with smaller sizes printed on them. We at FFF say, get over it and *love your bod!*

3. **INVEST IN A THREE-WAY MIRROR.** As we'll illustrate further in Chapter 9, nothing will help you finesse your fine points more. As one legendary fashion stylist once said, get naked, *stand before the mirror*, and be brutally honest with yourself. And designer Michael Kors said this not long ago on TV: You might as well look at your backside, he recommended, because "everyone else is." He has taken his recommendation even further, saying that those starkly lit dressing rooms we hate so much aren't half bad—after all, we see ourselves clearly and can make small but key adjustments from there.

4. **WEAR SOLID COLORS.** We're not saying, dear reader, avoid every print and pattern you see, just know that loud patterns, bright color mixes, and a hodgepodge of prints will always make you look heavier.

5. **MAINTAIN ONE FOCAL POINT.** The observer's eye will go wherever you tell it to—so if you have great legs and a thick middle and you wear a

short skirt, the eye will go to your asset. It's not accidental that stars, especially in the music world, dye their hair showy colors so our eyes go to the top and not to their sometimes heavier lower regions.

6. **CHOOSE ROLE MODELS THAT WORK FOR YOU.** Rather than model yourself after rail-thin runway models or movie stars who may starve themselves for a role, choose role models who have *body types like yours* and who have done a good job of assessing their assets and finessing the body parts they're less fond of. You'll feel a lot better that way.

7. **DON'T BE A FASHION VICTIM.** Some of us used to adore eyeballing celebs in sexy bias-cut dresses—until we realized that this unforgiving body-hugger looks good on almost no one else; it makes even the flattest tummy look bigger than it is; and your ass will never pass. Want more? See how great the average lass looks in the oh-so-popular pencil skirt. And whenever our style team expert, *Wall Street Journal* Senior Special Writer Teri Agins, sees one of the many unfortunates mistakenly wearing low-rise jeans, she says she thinks, "fashion victim." So *listen to yourself*, know you're beautiful, and know it's OK, as Agins suggests, to sit out a trend. We do.

8. **THE BODY TYPE VORTEX IS WIDE, WIDE, WIDE.** That's right. Ever since J. Lo, Beyoncé, and many others, rail thin is no longer truly in—not in *real life*. And certainly not with men . . . or us!

9. **TALK TO YOURSELF.** If your programming says, "I'm fat," change it to "I'm beautiful." Say it ten times a day in front of the mirror. We promise you, it works!

10. **FIT IS IT.** We've said it before—and we'll say it again. Nothing will make your body a showstopper more than *wearing clothes that fit*—and as Agins will tell you, many of the "universal sizes" you pick up in your favorite shop still need tweaking. Get thee a really good tailor—and that may mean someone better than your local dry cleaner.

And now, our complete Full Frontal Fashion Top Ten love-yourself guide to looking Fit & Flawless—and also stylish:

HIP HIP HOORAY

Nothing makes a woman more womanly than lush hips (and even a sizeable butt)—it's just too bad most of us don't buy it. (Men do, as *Glamour*'s executive fashion editor-at-large Suze Yalof Schwartz notes). That's why we have a few good hip-tips for you, the ladies among us:

1. **MAKE SURE YOU BALANCE YOUR JEANS.** By that we mean that if your jeans are tight on top (and they don't have to be jeans), make sure they're either flared or boot-cut to create an even picture. Otherwise, you're all thighs.

2. **WEAR VERTICAL STRIPES.** They will make you *look slimmer*.

3. **WEAR SKIRTS OR DRESSES.** They tend to be *more body beautifying* than pants and, as Agins advises, A-lines or modified flares (think trumpets) work a lot better than anything too narrow.

4. **KEEP IT CLEAN.** Too many pockets and details do a big butt, hips, and tummy make.

5. **WEAR A LONGER JACKET.** A little coverage isn't a bad thing.

6. **WEAR BRIGHT COLORS ON TOP.** As Yalof says, it will *draw the eye up to your finer points*; neckline detail does the same thing.

As for big-hip blunders, Agins says, say no to stretch jeans. "There are fashions and styles you just *have to* sit out," she says once again. And *Glamour*'s Schwartz, a big-time Fit & Flawless expert, adds: *Never* wear a shirt that ends where your saddle bags begin. "It widens your shape."

ARMED AND LANGUOROUS

For better or worse, our well-educated style team knows that most women hate—we repeat *hate*—their arms. Even Schwartz, whom we consider to be *très* stylish and slim, says of the skinny arms she longs for, "I've had dreams about them my whole life." What we know is that you need to learn to love them. And we'll add a few incisive inside-the-beltway pointers:

1. **GO STRAPLESS.** As Schwartz says, it shows off your shoulders, which are the only body part that never gets fat. The style icon for this awareness is without a doubt designer Donna Karan, who has been designing to **accentuate our shoulders** and collarbones for years. This way, the eye goes high. If you are not comfortable sharing your arms, by all means follow our next step (I know a lot of us do!).

2. **WRAP IT UP.** We love little bolero-style sweaters or shrugs or even cropped cardigans that cover the upper arms and leave everything else open to the eye—you can wear them day, night, and on the best of dates.

3. **GO SHEER.** Movie stars do it all the time—wear clothes with sheer or "illusion fabric" where they don't want to be fully exposed—and the arms are one key region. As Agins says, illusion fabric **shows off skin** while smoothing you out, sort of like a great pair of pricey nude pantyhose for the arms.

4. **WEAR LONG SLEEVES.** It's obvious, it works like a dream.

Your biggest arm error? "We let them show!" says Agins only half-jokingly. In place of sleeveless, she says, there's always the sheer scarf as a fall-back instant cover-up. And from our pro Schwartz: A tank neckline always makes your arms look bigger. Opt instead for a shoulder baring halter or a crew with short or long sleeves. Finally, we're not preaching, mind you, but nothing works better than lifting a few lightweight hand weights a few times a week!

WAIST NOT, WANT NOT

If you think you're too thick in the middle, you figure you should do all you can to cover it up. But, we say, hold your wardrobe horses. Susan Barbash, a stylish buddy of ours who admits to being a bit self-conscious about her mid-section, wears body-revealing tops—say, a halter in taupe or a shirt that ends strategically an inch or so below her waist—to draw the eye either upward or to create the appearance of shape—without ever looking dowdy or less than chic. She's also careful to tailor her tops for that illusion of shapeliness, and she's careful with color—if she sports taupe on top, she's likely to wear a similar shade on the bottom to give her a long, lean, shapely line.

A few other rules of the waist-not game:

1. **GO FOR FITTED TUNICS AND/OR LONGER TOPS.** The best have *detail at the neckline* to draw the eye away from the waist and are slightly flow-y on the top to prevent unnecessary tugging and pulling. Remember: Too tight will never be right. And: If the fit is flawed, get thee to a good tailor.

2. **GATHER IT UP.** Little is more flattering to you with the thicker mid-section than a shirt that is slightly gathered to *show off your shape* without being

so tight you're revealing sausage rolls (or shall we say back fat?).

3. **OPT FOR WRAP STYLES.** If you don't want to look boy-shaped (which a thick middle can do), a wrap-style is great, says Schwartz. If you have a big belly, however, skip it.

4. **WEAR IT OUT.** As our buddy Barbash notes, you can always choose a top that *doesn't need tucking*—just make sure, as Schwartz notes, that it ends right at the hip bone.

5. **BE A WISE JEANS SHOPPER.** If they cut into your midriff or lower midriff region and create front, back, and/or side bulge (and you don't have to be big for that!), don't buy them. Instead, buy jeans that are a bit too big—they may fit well as they are or you may need to have them altered.

6. **BELT IT—WITH CARE!** Even our style team splits on this one. Agins says maybe if it's skinny and your top has vertical ribbing, but handle with care—and if you have a big tummy, don't!

Can you mess up with your mid-section? Yep, warns Agins—by wearing a top that is too tight. "A lot of women are walking around with an extra piece of meat showing," she says honestly. Finally, we on the FFF squad say, assuredly, nix the horizontal stripes.

GOING THIGH HIGH

The Thigh-Master-ers among us know that nothing bothers us more than simply putting on a few thigh pounds and hearing that song that thighs sing when they rub against one another, or stepping into a dimly lit dressing room to try on bathing suits and feeling depressed as we watch our accumulating cellulite in bright light. So we'll start there:

1. **BUY A BATHING SUIT WITH HIGH LEG HOLES.** And make sure you also buy a pareo. Our FFF style team absolutely loves this combo (as we told you in Chapters 4 and 5) for everything from lunch at the beach to dinner or even Black-Tie Optional. It was Agins who used—and continues to use—her favorite pareo as an evening wrap.

2. **BUY FLAT-FRONT PANTS.** As Suze Yalof Schwartz will tell you, jeans with pleats of any kind will make a thigh disaster scene. So make sure yours are flat front so your *body line is long and lean*, with no interruptions;

3. **WEAR A DRESS.** If you really feel your thighs are too big for pants, don't wear them.

4. **WEAR DARK COLORS ON THE BOTTOM.** We've said it before, we say it again.

5. **GO CALF-LENGTH.** You can always draw the eye down and away from your thighs; Agins suggests, too, a trumpet skirt.

6. **ACCESSOR-EYES.** You can also *draw the eye up* with accessories—for example, a great pin or print scarf. As Agins says, "Most people only see you from the torso up."

7. **GO OPAQUE.** Darker hose elongate your legs.

8. **SIT DOWN.** Any stylist worth his or her celeb clients

will tell you: No outfit is thigh-complete until you've seen what comes up when you take your seat.

Now, a few FFF Wardrobe Warnings on thighs: Heavy fabrics, especially when sported head-to-toe—we're still pondering the bevy of celebs who were photographed in top-down red velvet at holiday time—are a thigh-expanding no-no. Ditto, says Schwartz, for wearing white on the bottom—and pleats, unless, says Agins, they're stitched together, especially at the hip. And minis may not be for you, either.

PETIT CHIC

The tiniest titans among us can get along pretty well with a few important body-beautiful tips:

1. **WEAR LONGER PANTS.** Our point: *Avoid cropped pants* at all costs.

2. **WEAR CLOTHES THAT FIT YOU.** Too big is too much—even if you spent $5,000 on your outfit.

3. **BECOME A MONOCHROMATIC DRESSER.** One shade will give you one long, lean line rather than slice you in half, all of which will make you look taller and slimmer.

4. **KEEP IT CROPPED ON TOP.** Nothing flatters the petite shape more than a *properly fitted* cropped top or sweater or jacket.

5. **SAVOR SHORTER HEM-LINES.** Too long in a skirt can pull you down. So be sure to stand in front of a full-length mirror and take the measure of your entire body. If you look best in shorter skirts, wear them—no matter the fashion.

6. **WEAR HEELS.** We're on the fence about this one, but it's the consensus of our FFF style team pros. Obviously, a heel will make you look taller and *leaner (and sexier)*. And as Agins says, there are a lot of comfortable heels out there women can wear.

A final FFF Wardrobe Warning: Avoid shoes with ankle straps (you'll either look like Little Orphan Annie or stubby); and again, cropped pants are our number-one skip-it trick for the petite among us, along with boxy shapes or jackets that are too long.

TALL IS ALL

As *Glamour*'s Suze Yalof Schwartz says, the tall and lean among us can wear just about anything they want. So here goes the tall-is-all tip game (and we admit to being a bit jealous!) with a list of all that you can get away with:

1. **BOLD PATTERNS AND PRINT MIXES.** Yep—you're the only body type who can get away with it!

2. **BIGGER ACCESSORIES.** Ditto. You can sport the grandest of pendants, the biggest of tote bags, and the longest of chandeliers without fear.

3. **FULLER SLEEVES.** They can blow in the breeze— without making your arms look like birthday balloons.

4. **STRETCH JEANS.** Low-rise jeans were invented for your body type.

5. **RUFFLED TOPS.** Go get it, girl! Because most of us would look like a goat about to be sheared.

6. **MINISKIRTS AND FLAT SHOES.** That says it all.

Tall really is all but you can flub your finessing. Don't buy clothes that are too big because they only make you look bigger, warns Schwartz. She also warns against too many bright colors if you're indeed very tall. "At-six-feet-four, bright green might look like the Jolly Green Giant." And, Agins says, if you happen to be big and tall as opposed to not so big and tall, big prints "give you a sloppy look." Grooming is also particularly important if there's a lot of you to look at. And, finally, if you're in this glorious group, we say go for a soft duster or stylish three-quarter-length cover-up under which you can sport a tighter top and bottom—it's chic and neat over clothes and/or under a heavier coat.

BUST MUSTS

A note to our e-mailer at the very beginning of this chapter: *Glamour*'s Suze Yalof Schwartz says, very much in sync with you, "With a small bust you can wear the deepest-plunging necklines, whereas if you have a bigger bust, you look like a slut." Susan Grossman, nineteen, a beautiful southern California college student, notes that although she is clearly curvy (and not necessarily big-busted), she avoids low-cuts tops, too, because "then you have to worry about your cleavage." As we've told you before, one reason that certain celebrities—think Elizabeth Hurley or Jennifer Lopez—look so smashing in revealing clothes is that they are not terribly big on top.

That said, nothing is more confidence-building than taking the best care of your beautiful curves. So here, our favorite bust musts, whether you want to show off or minimize:

1. **WEAR A BANDEAU NECKLINE.** Straight across hides or *minimizes a large bust*—just make sure it has a built-in shelf bra if it's a flimsier tube top; a square neckline is fine, too, as Schwartz notes.

2. **BUY A GOOD BRA OR BRAS.** Most of us are still hanging out in the same bra we wore in high school. We might as well tell you that's an FFF Wardrobe Warning of major proportions (and we do mean major). Go and *get yourself fitted* for the proper bra(s) for every situation and type of clothing in your closet. There has never been a time with more choices and solutions, whether you want to minimize or maximize, or neither.

3. **GO COLLARLESS.** If you're broad in the chest, don't wear clothes with giant collars.

4. **KEEP IT CLEAN ON TOP.** Emblems, logos, and other embellishments at mid-chest make you look like a mess.

5. **SINGLE-BREASTED IS BEST.** As Suze Yalof Schwartz notes, double-breasted means what it says.

6. **KEEP IT SMALL ON THE BOTTOM.** As Schwartz also notes, going big on the bottom means you'll look bigger on top.

7. **IF YOU'RE SMALL-BUSTED,** our pros say, nothing beats a push-up bra. Nothing.

Finally, as Teri Agins so rightfully adds, nothing is a bigger bust blunder than a bra that doesn't cover enough of you. "I had meat hanging out on the sides!" she admits. You can also add "too tight" to that, so that one can see "meat rolls" in the back or bra straps binding.

FFF WARDROBE WARNING

Most of us are still hanging out in the same bra we wore in high school. We might as well tell you this is an FFF Wardrobe Warning of major proportions (and we do mean major!). Go and get yourself fitted for the proper bra(s) for every situation and type of clothing in your closet. There has never been a time with more choices and solutions, whether you want to minimize or maximize, or neither.

UNDERSTANDING UNDERGARMENTS

As one of our FFF style team members told us recently (and we agree)—you've got to suck it in! By that we mean make use of the essentials of the smoothed-out, panty-line-free, tummy-tucked-in, well-shaped butt of a world we live in. As Teri Agins exclaimed when we first talked to her about this, "Foundations . . . I'm telling you, they're HUGE . . . I don't like to jiggle!" This includes body-shapers (some with special attention to the butt or tummy or thighs, or torso or waistline), control-top panty hose (with control tops for the tummy and/or thighs, or calf-length and footless for a smoother thigh line); full panties with stretch to hold you in; even pants or skirts with built-in liners to make you look chic and sleek and streamlined. And, of course, unlike the girdles of your mom's or grandmom's day, you can find examples of these essentials that are not only soft to the touch but comfortable to wear.

And as Jeffrey Kalinsky so strongly points out in our Dating chapter (Chapter 6), nothing is more important for invisible panty-lines than wearing a thong. And Schwartz adds, if, like some of us, too, you're scared to wear one at first, try it for a week . . . "then it's like wearing nothing." And, yes, a few fashionable folks we know do wear no underwear, usually with a pair of control-top hose or a shaper that has a built-in cotton crotch. As Agins says, it's even more armor against those thigh-lines!

Our number-one FFF Wardrobe Warning on undergarments comes from Kalinsky: Make sure that your thong doesn't show when you bend over (watch those low-rise jeans!). Check yourself out first and if it does, make sure you're wearing something to cover it. Number two is an insider secret: If you find a pair of control-tops or a shaper you love, you can always buy them in bulk online. Our exuberant expert Teri Agins does. Number three: If your strapless bra is falling down or flattens you out (as we know can happen all too often), and you're busy tugging and pulling, listen to our stylish college student Susan Grossman. "You won't have fun, so why wear it?" she says. In Grossman's case, she opts for one without the oh-so-popular overload of padding and shaping.

ACE YOUR FACE

Your best body-beautiful trick is to ace your face. It's the best place for the eye to go—and whether you like it or not, it will ultimately be the centerpiece of your style. Agins says your first must-buy is without a doubt a 5x magnification makeup mirror to help prevent streaky makeup, to conceal dark circles properly, and to get those stray brow hairs in check.

After that, know that your best facial accessory is beautiful skin—so keep it healthy by using a high-quality cleanser, a moisturizer, and a sunscreen with an SPF of at least 30; also be sure to drink a lot of water. As one style team member noted, beautiful skin is *really* what sets J. Lo apart.

Our number three facial fix? Agins says, don't forget beautiful teeth. "Teeth are 80 percent of your face," she insists. "I see again and again people who need to get their teeth cleaned." Finally, you can also highlight and downplay your features using makeup—think making a nose smaller, lips bigger, cheekbones more defined. If you want a lesson, your best bet is a scheduled appointment at your favorite department-store counter. If you don't have a favorite, start shopping around now.

Next comes your hair. As Yalof Schwartz points out, how you wear it can have a major effect on your flawless meter. Big hair, for instance, makes your face look smaller; straight

FFF WARDROBE WARNING

"A lot of people have bad haircuts," says *Wall Street Journal* Senior Special Writer Teri Agins. "You see a lot of bad streaks and dye jobs, especially with blonde and highlights. If you're going to go that route, you're going to need to spend time and money keeping it up."

hair bigger. As Sasha, an expert stylist at the Gerard Bollei Salon in New York, notes, your cut can reduce the appearance of a weak or sagging chin or keep a round, full one from looking like a big ball; it can help give you the look of a longer neck, bigger eyes, or more pronounced cheekbones.

Finally, a Wardrobe Warning from Agins: "A lot of people have bad hair cuts," she says, adding, "You see a lot of bad streaks and dye-jobs, especially with blonde and high-lights. If you're going to go that route, you're going to need to spend time and money keeping it up."

BEING CHIC-SHAPE

Whether you're pear or hourglass or have a swimmer's body, the ultimate purpose of dressing the body beautiful is to create as much of an hourglass as you can (see our tips in Chapter 10). Or, as Agins calls it, "a pretty hourglass." Ideally, this can mean a nice pretty sweater with a boat or scoop neck, or modified wrap-top, and a skirt with just a little room at the hips (think modified dirndl) or with embellishment at the hemline (think trumpet or flounced).

Here, a few rules for the figure-eights among us:

1. **TIGHT IS MIGHT.** We're not saying suck it in so you can't breathe, but in general, as evening-wear designer Randolph Duke once told us, *tighter looks better* than loose and baggy—even if you think you're carrying a few extra pounds.

2. **KEEP IT LIGHTWEIGHT.** Go for clothes made from lightweight seasonless fabric—and shop with that in mind (they're also great for climate to cli-mate travel, as we told you in Chapter 4). This will *slim you out* and make you look head-to-toe chic.

3. **BLACK IS BACK.** Not that it went away (actually it did for a season or so), not that we don't just adore color—but if you do go with head-to-toe black, it will focus the eye on your figure-eight shape;

4. **CARVE OUT YOUR TOPPER.** As we told you in our Casual chapter (Chapter 5), we all look like oversized sausages in extra-long coats, especially quilted ones or shapeless raincoats. If you are going long in the coat, make sure it's *narrow in shape*.

Can you go wrong with your chic shape in any way? Yes. By not keeping an eye on your tucking action. If tucking your top in will add to a smooth hourglass, go for it; if it creates a bulge or your top won't stay tucked in, either don't tuck it or find a top that fits you and can be worn on the outside with ease and comfort (as our stylish buddy Susan Barbash told us).

Host HINT

★ Our intrepid host, Rebecca Budig, has learned from years of experience that the best way to dress in style for her body type (in this case petite) is to avoid impulse buying. "I never impulse buy," she says emphatically, "because I've learned that it's in that spur-of-the-moment gush of wardrobe enthusiasm that I make nearly all of my body-type mistakes. I'll walk away from it, then I'll go back and try it on . . . but I won't impulse buy."

10

the top ten
FFF FIT & FLAWLESS DOS AND DON'TS

DO

Wear flat-front pants—if you have big hips.

Mix prints and patterns at will—if you're tall.

Sport comfortable heels—if you're petite and chic.

Look for a great fitted tunic—if you have a thick middle.

Wear a bandeau or square neckline—if you're big-busted.

DON'T

Tuck it in—if it won't stay put or your saddle bags show.

Wear ultra-bright colors—if you're really big and tall.

Wear baggy clothes—at all, and especially if you're small.

Wear ultra-stretchy jeans—if you're thick in the hips.

Go low-rise—if you have midriff bulge.

CHAPTER EIGHT

HOW TO SHOP

Dear Full Frontal Fashion:

I used to live in a big city where I could find great sales on really trendy things—but now that I'm in a smaller town, all I can find are basics. Can you give me a road map to the insider stuff?

CLOTHES ROADIE

what comes to mind immediately are Web sites—Lazar Shopping, TopButton, and Daily Candy. They gives us the scoop, city by city, of the best sample sales, other Web sites and/or fashion finds and shopping events.

And now to the meat of our chapter: As Teri Agins, the senior special writer for the *Wall Street Journal,* has told us, the biggest change in the retail landscape is that we have so many choices—both clothing and store choices—that we barely know what to do anymore. Moreover, it used to be that we all piled in the car and mom drove us to the nearest department store or boutique. Well, these days we not only have choices galore, but how we shop is as big a part of our identity as what we wear.

So to cut through the shopping clutter, here, a guide to traveling the slippery slope of shopping:

VINTAGE

Some shopping personalities, like fashion types, are more involved (even emotionally) with fashion than others. Think the Vintage Shopper or Eccentric Personality. Among us on the Full Frontal Fashion style squad are seriously devoted Pucci collectors, sleepless seekers of old Levi's denim (circa 1900), and scouts for that long-lost couture find—at the moment, Courrèges.

As our celebrity stylist, James Aguiar, notes a bit facetiously, "This is the person who would rather eat nails than go into something like Banana Republic or the Gap . . . Basically, she would never set foot in a mainstream store. She's a one-of-a-kind girl and proud of it."

Indeed, the Vintager loves the compelling quality of the search and the research, and she loves the fulfillment of the find. For instance, on a foray into Urban Outfitters the other day, we met Megan Cuomo, a fashion-school student, who had just found a very pricey designer clutch at the

Salvation Army for $4.99. And fashion-fulfilled she was! Vintage-hounds like Cuomo also love the connection to higher-quality clothes that may not otherwise be found so easily and inexpensively nowadays; and, perhaps most important, the connection to the trends.

Indeed, if you are taking the vintage plunge, even for the first time, *Elle* magazine's fashion news director Anne Slowey suggests starting out by learning the trends—for it's the trends that vintage stores will stock in heavy supply. So if your favorite designer runway show, like those featured on Full Frontal Fashion each season, focuses on sixties retro bohemian, know that this is what your favorite vintage shop will stock, too. And, know, too, as Slowey explained, that it may take time to understand how to identify vintage trends in order to shop for them in the first place.

Finally, as all vintage devotees know, while you're focusing on finding, say, the perfect vintage tunic circa 1975, the world's foremost designers are scouring the world of vintage for the trends that you will see on the runways each season—so you, the vintage shopper, are *always* in the loop. And if you really work hard at it—ahead of it, too.

So what are your best bets in the world of vintage? Without a doubt, we say opt for a coat (it doesn't have to be a famous label, and the quality is likely to beat the basics at your neighborhood chain). We also strongly suggest antique jewelry—even our Classic Personality (not usually a Vintage Shopper), Joan Kaner, the senior vice president and fashion director at Neiman Marcus, can't resist weekends at her favorite flea market collecting jewelry.

So, can you blunder on the vintage trail? A number of the Classics on our FFF style council say yes. They warn against everything from deodorant stains to clothing of questionable provenance. Many of them can't stand the very thought of putting on something old. We say, please do make sure the clothes are clean and in good shape.

BOUTIQUE

The Boutique Shopper is one step removed from the Vintage hound in that she, too, considers herself a member of a private, somewhat insiderly and very trend-driven club. But unlike the Vintage Shopper, the Boutique Shopper enjoys the snob appeal of shopping at her favorite in-the-know hot spot. "With the boutique shopper, it's not only what you buy but where you're seen buying it," explains Aguiar. "It's about being scene, so to speak . . . that's why you see so many celebrities photographed at the coolest boutiques—you don't see them photographed at Wal-Mart."

Most of our FFF high-style team members are avid Boutique Shoppers (perhaps combined with another shopping type). As *Elle*'s Slowey indicates, she loves the unique merchandise, the service (they do remember you if you come back often), and, as only an editor can tell you, the way the clothes are "edited." You don't have to go through twenty outfits by forty designers—the store owner has done the "editing" for you with the idea that you're getting the best (most stylish) of the bunch. And, of course, that's exactly the same job that magazine editors perform every day.

So what's your best choice when you stop at the boutique? Without hesitation, we say a unique dress. But be forewarned: Contrary to what a number of experts say, boutique shopping is not truly one-of-a-kind shopping; rather, it is niche-specific shopping—thus, the very "in" boutiques, say, Scoop or Calypso in New York, specialize in clothes for a young, trendy customer. It is not all things to all people. So, if you're not a member of that trendy club, this may not be the place for you.

MALL

Ask our expert team member, Mandi Norwood, the editor-in-chief of *Shop Etc.*, why she's a true mall lover and she'll actually get excited. She loves the social element—going with her family, taking a break to get something to eat, then starting up again. And she loves stocking up on basics—underwear, socks, lingerie, tees. And like other pros including the *Wall Street Journal*'s Teri Agins, she advises picking your mall wisely, because not all malls are alike. Norwood, like Slowey, also recommends buying what you love and look good in, even if it does cost a few dollars more and isn't on sale. For all of our pros, it's not the money, honey. Ever.

Indeed, Norwood and Slowey do a lot of shopping at what we're calling the newfangled all-American mall—not just your pile-in-the-car strip center, but the stylish stores that are chock-a-block and sophisticated—from Coach to Banana Republic ("Banana" to our team) to higher-end outlets like Prada and the new Michael Kors shop. And in these shops, it is the service that Norwood and Slowey adore. As Norwood says, the folks at Prada call her whenever her favorite white shirt and black pants come in; they notify her of sales. And it is true, dear reader, that you do not have to buy anything terribly pricey to get this kind of attention.

With this in mind, of course, "mall" stores like H&M and Target have entered the designer game (with plenty more to come!) so that you, no matter your income, can stop in for a great retail find. So, what's best for the mall maven? We love the new designer finds from lower-priced stores, like Lagerfeld for H&M or Mizrahi for Target (we saw an evening gown at one such store that cost under a hundred

Host HINT

★ We love the idea of bulking up on basics. As our clever host, Rebecca Budig, says, if you find something basic you love, buy at least two of them. Or why not three?

dollars and looked like it cost thousands). We can't wait to see more designers enter the fray. We also love malls for handbags, especially the everyday totes that you can now find in chic, stylish colors. And we love the idea of bulking up on basics. As our clever host Rebecca Budig says, if you find something basic that you love, buy at least two of them.

WEB

Let's begin with a very hip Web-meister we ran across last week: Sheila Petrowski, a nineteen-year-old student at a college near Los Angeles who became a real pro at shopping for trendy clothes online, because the boarding school she attended was miles away from any half-decent boutiques. She still orders her favorite fashion jeans; she orders Juicy Couture; and she even goes so far as to order dresses—but only if they're stretch tube dresses, so her size issues don't come into play. And she always tells her fellow Web shoppers this: If you're buying a non-basic item, make sure you order from sites where the clothes are shown on models—that way you can see the cut. She buys all of her shirts that way. Finally, like other meisters in our midst, she takes a few risks—and doesn't mind returning the occasional item.

We have another hot Web type on tap: Jamie Burmester, a singer/performance artist (and Eccentric Fashion Personality who entertains under the stage name "Scandal"), who lives by her eBay finds. The most recent was a great silk jacket we spotted her in—beautifully embroidered and, as she will tell you, a steal for only $19.99.

And we have yet another group: The shoppers who don't want to visit those starkly lit, depressing dressing rooms (brick and mortify, you might say). They prefer to go at it alone at home, as do some of us for whom size or sizing might be an issue. No item of clothing is more potentially popular as an online purchase than the bathing suit—after all, you can now "image" yourself in private and even customize. Our pal Petrowski shops for jeans online because, she says, she can size herself extra-tall in a way the stores can't.

Finally, we have our somewhat safe Web shoppers (OK, we're in that group) who use the Web for basics and for anything where size is an absolute known quantity. Agins shops online for pantyhose and she buys the designer skirts she knows well and loves.

So how do you start? If you shop for just two items from your home, let them be something casual to begin with (say, an ultra-stylish hoodie and a great pair of track pants); you can also go for a bathing suit. We love the two-piece, boy-leg styles (if your body type allows).

FFF WARDROBE WARNING

If you're buying a non-basic item on the Web, make sure you look at sites where the clothes are shown on models—that way you can see the cut. Our hip pal, Sheila Petrowski, buys her trendy shirts that way.

BUDGET-CONSCIOUS

OK. We just love a bargain. Our producer pal Kim Sunshine, who is an avid Budget-Conscious Shopper, captures the essential element of the truly successful: She never ever, *ever* pays retail. And she has all the other elements, too: a love of the hunt; a good eye (which you can develop the more you peruse magazines and watch TV shows like *Full Frontal Fashion*); and the knowledge that you can't just drop by a great discount store (think Loehmann's or Daffy's or, in the New York area, the mega-fave Century 21) one time and expect to strike it rich. As the *Journal*'s Agins says, she stops in all the time (to her nearest "Century's," as she puts it); that way she learns what comes in when, and she also spots the best finds before anyone else gets to them. And all of our pros do find, eventually, great designer finds.

But be forewarned: Buy a discount item only if you feel good in it—a bargain price is not a reason to buy. But the great discount shops that are in fashion capitals—think New York and maybe Los Angeles—often are sent the most fashionable stuff. Nothing makes a better travel sideline on a visit to one of these cities than budget-conscious shopping.

And this from Agins: Don't take the tags off! She sometimes sleeps on a find and then takes it back. Be sure to check the return policy.

INSIDER SECRET

The great discount shops that are in fashion capitals—think New York or maybe Los Angeles—often are sent the most fashionable stuff. Nothing makes a better travel sideline when visiting one of these cities than budget-conscious shopping—and taking home that great $1000-plus designer find that cost you less than $100.

EMERGENCY SHOPPER

We hate to admit it, but among our ranks we count three Emergency Shoppers—that is, those of us who wait until the heel breaks off the shoe before we go out and get a new pair. The excuse is always a lack of time, but Emergency we are nonetheless. So if you are one of us, we say this: Make sure you have a lineup of good nearby Emergency stores on tap (some are great at last-minute help). That way if the potential love of your life asks you out at five p.m., you know just where you can get that great sexy V-neck and skirt by five-thirty. And, as our pros do, you may want to line up a big specialty store for emergencies, because the assortment is larger.

Also, you can do what another member of our team did—the night before she was to go to Milan for the fashion shows, she called the personal shopping department at her favorite specialty store and asked them to put her together head-to-toe. They did and beautifully. In addition, you may want to identify Emergency choices that are open Sundays (this particular personal shopping department stop was for a Monday morning flight).

As you can imagine, this type of shopping does have it pitfalls (and lots of detractors on our Style squad). Joan Kaner, Neiman Marcus's revered fashion director, an admitted Emergency type and a Uniform Dresser Fashion Personality, often finds that her nearby stores are out of black, her number-one color pick. What's left are strange styles in ultra-bright colors. There are, however, stores that do restock their basics—think the great V-neck and the skirt—even though the first-of-the-season finds will be gone. We do suggest you plan ahead.

DEPARTMENT AND SPECIALTY STORE

Fashion insiders always distinguish between department and specialty stores—for instance, a specialty store like Bergdorf Goodman or Barneys or Saks or Neiman Marcus doesn't carry hard goods (think large electronic devices), while many department stores do. For your shopping purposes and ours, however, we think of them as one—with a few exceptions. The Department and Specialty Store Shopper loves one-stop shopping. This is not your lover of the hunt or even the fulfillment of the find. This is someone far more time- and function-driven. That said, many of our team members, including James Aguiar, Joan Kaner (who works for one such store), and Mandi Norwood, love the service, particularly at specialty stores where the sales professionals get to know you and call you when there's a sale or your favorite items come in.

And much like the newfangled "mall" stores, these stores do carry designer lines and do edit to some degree. But, as the Department Store Shopper who loves fashion knows, you do need to pick your specialty store carefully as the "edit" will differ, depending on the store's audience. Thus, if the runways are showing micro-minis, one store might be featuring classic pants instead; if the catwalks are filled with stilettos, another might be heavy on chunkier heels. Ditto for decorative evening versus simple evening. Remember, for big stores that do big business (and for plenty of us, too), runway is not reality. It's usually icing on the fashion cake.

As our pros know, there is a big comeback in the department and specialty store world and many of us who maybe didn't shop at these spots before are heading there in droves. They're giving us more and better cafés in which to eat and hang out, and more entertainment—think personal appearances and trunk shows (if you've never gone and had a designer get on all fours to hem your skirt, give it a try!). But most of all, we go for what no other type of shopping can beat: shoes (the assortments are chic and large) and makeup (it's the best place by far to test the waters, which we recommend every season, by appointment, at your favorite counter, and if you don't have one, just go with your gut. And as we told you, you don't even have to buy anything—just learn what looks good.)

CATALOG

Catalog shoppers love their privacy; they love the read (after all, these days the most sophisticted stores are putting out catalogs that resemble the leading fashion mags); they love searching out basics they don't have to try on. And we all at least know about the J.Crew catalog or that absolute staple, the Victoria's Secret catalog.

Catalog shopping has also become the heartbeat of the Combo Shopper, or the newfangled fashionista who reads the catalog, then drops by the store, and then buys any way she chooses.

Finally, as *Shop Etc.* Editor-in-Chief Mandi Norwood notes, there's a more cutting-edge Catalog Shopper showing up these days who does buy stylish merchandise from newer, trendier catalogs that she doesn't necessarily feel the need to try on. Norwood herself buys hot-looking shoes that approximate ones she knows fit well—and feels that it has worked out well.

So, we say, if you do go for catalog picks, we still love casual as our number-one category— a great jacket that's more than a barn jacket or a windbreaker; a pair of rain boots in fun patterns or colors. In addition to basics, of course—think a big stack of rainbow Tees. You can't live without them and you don't have to leave home, either.

FFF WARDROBE WARNING

Catalogs can change their styling and, worse, lower the quality of their fabric. If you receive the same item you've always loved and suddenly the cloth feels scratchy, return it and shop someplace else. That, and complaining, is the only way these companies will change their acts.

OUTLET

Our producer pal Kim Sunshine is a Budget-Conscious Shopper
and an expert Outlet Shopper, too. She picks her outlets carefully; she makes regular forays without a list in hand; she also
has an expert eye (you can develop yours, as we noted); and
she does locate incredible finds: $1000-plus Prada boots for
a song; Pucci-style skirts for next to nothing; sleek turtlenecks from Donna Karan that are both stylish and timeless.
Which brings us to another good outlet asset: Our pal is not
a trend-monger. She will buy those $1,000-plus Prada boots
with the chunkier heel and wear them when stilettos
are in style—and they still, by the way, look great—paired
sleekly with the turtleneck from way back when, and the skirt
from last year.

She also has one more expert outlet qualification we
just can't explain: a near-fanatical love of bargain-hunting runs in her family (OK, maybe it is hereditary!).

Our suggestions for the first-time Outlet Shopper: Make a day of it and go with
friends and/or family. You can break up, visit your favorite stores, or explore, and
then meet up for lunch and start out again. Look for clothes that may not
be the hot-off-the-runway styles, but are usefully stylish nonetheless. A
seasonless raincoat is a good idea. But be forewarned: Many of our pros note
that you may not be getting top-of-the-season merchandise; moreover, some merchandise is created specifically for the outlet and isn't a leftover from the designer line; and
finally, what's left over isn't necessarily what's always the most chic.

COUPLES SHOPPER

We couldn't resist this category because wherever we go these days, both men and women are buying clothes together—at the local shoe store, at the jeans outlet, at specialty stores with areas for him and areas for her. And, of course, the old saw still applies: that you, dear female reader, are probably going with him for his clothes most of the time with not much, if any, time in his schedule for you; and when he does go with you, he likely has 10 percent of your fashion patience (why don't we just buy it and leave?). One of our top Full Frontal Fashion pros figures that men accompany their women when there's something more than a buy in mind—like watching you try on good-butt jeans. Or, as Joan Kaner of Neiman's added, men sometimes accompany women when the women are trying on dresses for a social occasion that may involve his boss, or a situation that's truly socially significant for him.

OK, enough of the fashion male-bashing. The ultimate Couples shop is the venture out for an engagement ring. All we had to do was visit Tiffany & Co. to see the lineup of duos! (Say good-bye to your mom's etiquette that it was his job to surprise you.) And our advice? As our Style Squad member Jeffrey Kalinksy told you about date clothes, educate him from the beginning about your love of jewelry.

the top ten
FFF HOW TO SHOP
DOS AND DON'TS

DO

Do bargain shop—but never buy just because it's on sale.

Do shop when you travel—especially to a big city with a great assortment of hot-off-the-runway clothes.

Do make a day of it—especially if you're visiting the outlets.

Do make a boutique your means—if you want to make the scene.

Do Web shop—if you're far from trendy stores.

DON'T

Make just one visit to a discount store—it has to be a regular routine.

Emergency shop—without knowing your local last-minute stores.

Forget to pick up makeup—at a department or specialty store.

Be a trend-monger—if you're an outlet shopper, timelessness is best.

Web shop for a dress—unless it's classic and stretch.

CHAPTER NINE

EDITING
YOUR CLOSET

Dear Full Frontal Fashion:

You're not going to believe this, but I actually coach people on how to reduce stress in their lives. Yet, as my closest friends know, my own home is a sea of closet clutter—which is causing me some anxiety. Can you help me break through what is clearly resistance?

CLUTTER BUG

Editing your closet is a lot like packing the perfect suitcase (some of us would say it's a bit like dieting, too!). There is a perfect, ultimately simple path to perfection. But for largely psychological reasons, we dread the process as if it were a root canal. Jesse Garza, the creative director and part owner of Visual Therapy, the top-notch image consulting (including major clutter-clearing) business to the rich and famous (and some regular folks, too), says that our nearly lethal fear of editing out our no-good goods comes from our attachments. "Most of us just can't seem to let go," he says. Think the never-worn, ten-year-old leopard flats, the designer sale find we just couldn't resist but never wore, the handbag from five years ago that still has a zipper that doesn't work (and we haven't fixed) . . . even the dress from a trip to London when we were in high school.

Garza's well-worn advice? Be brutal, he says. That doesn't mean you have to toss the sentimental favorites, but it does mean you need to learn to let go step-by-step until (and we know this from experience) you become a pro. Then you can do it, one-two-three.

So, here, our well-edited ***Full Frontal Fashion* advice on editing, tossing, tweaking, and reorganizing the perfect at-home closet.**

THE PLAN

We think about it, we consider it, then we don't do it. Planning our editing ahead of time is very important. It gives us the hours and focus we need to do a great job. As Garza notes, when you do give yourself some time to plan, so much pent-up energy is released that new possibilities actually come into your life—that's how much and how hard we carry the burden of our clutter. Our host, Rebecca Budig, is a seriously organized closet pro. "It's like a cleansing," she says.

Moreover, as Garza explains: Editing is not a once-a-year activity (usually at year's end or as a New Year's resolution, come January). Rather, it is a year-round activity—get rid of that yellowing white shirt you left in the plastic the second you see it, and add in that perfect new one that makes your corporate business suit so sexy you just can't wait to leave the office.

In the meantime, establish a timetable for your plan: Leave one week maximum for your full closet edit (you can spread this over available time periods such as weekends if you prefer), but be sure to leave one full day at the beginning and handle the rest quickly within seven days total. In addition, we recommend quick seasonal shifts—putting those "inactive" summer shirts on the shelf and returning the "active" or "current" winter ones to the hangers, and vice versa.

So, here goes an easy plan for your edit-ification:

1. **DAY 1:** the Weeding

2. **DAYS 2–4:** the Seeding

3. **DAYS 5–7:** the Reorganization

And a few supplies to begin:

1. A legal pad and pen

2. A few regular garbage bags

THE WEEDING

This is what you leave that first full day for, and here's the one thing we at Full Frontal Fashion say you must do: Invite a good friend or family member to help you break through the resistance, keep on track, and give honest advice on what to toss. Also, make sure your weeding is comprehensive—think underwear, panty hose, socks, and beauty supplies, too.

1. **STEP ONE, DAY ONE:** The Easy Pull Out. *Take everything out of your closet that you no longer need.* As you do this, ask yourself the following key questions:

   - **Is it stained?** Pilling? Shiny from too much dry cleaning? If the answer is yes, it's a Toss.

   - **Is it torn?** If so, it's a Toss, too.

   - **Is it never worn?** Consider it a Toss or a Donation.

   - **Is it a mis-fit?** If it doesn't fit, toss it. And donate it if and only if it's clean, in good condition, and you know you can do it right away.

   - **Is it too old?** If the answer is even hesitatingly yes, it's a Must-Toss. An FFF Wardrobe Warning here: Old handbags are an organizational no-no. As Garza says, if you're keeping them from five years ago, don't. They will date your wardrobe instantly (and much more than other items). As for old bathing suits, they're an easy toss. You deserve a fresh one every year.

   - **Is it too bold?** Yes equals Toss. Example: If you're a Classic Fashion Personality and you have anything too Eccentric, it's time for a Toss.

   - **Is it a hit?** Do I feel good in it? Be very honest with yourself—you may want to mimic our style expert Jeffrey Kalinsky when he suggested asking, "Do I feel sassy?" Garza says just make sure you feel sexy. If so, save it for the Reorganization.

   - **Is it a keeper?** It is if the fabric is very high quality and it meets the qualifications above.

- **Is it a sleeper?** It is if you forgot you had it, it's timeless, and you suddenly rediscover it, as Garza states. A common example: something for a vacation trip, such as a pareo or oversized Ralph Lauren shirt that you forgot you had and now realize you can easily use. If it meets these qualifications, save it for the Reorganization (and wear it).

- **Is it a reaper?** Garza warns against filling boxes with goods we say we're going to sell on eBay or sell at a vintage shop because the energy we free up by tossing is a far greater return (it's like comparing losing twenty pounds to waiting until you lose twenty pounds to buy that next item). But we are willing to bend the rules a bit if you can make that move within seven days maximum and not do as one of our trusted team has done. She's still looking at her designated eBay box a year later!

- **Is it a multi-cycler?** One of the biggest changes in fashion is the length of the so-called fashion cycles—or how long it takes for a trend to come back around. It used to be five to seven years, but now the cycles have sped up. Not only that, thanks to the vintage boom, certain trends come around with some certainty—a good example is leopard—so you may want to save a few key pieces. But again, don't save handbags or shoes or anything that fits that is "yes" to our edit questions.

- **Is it a sentimental favorite?** If you still have the vinyl miniskirt from the sixties that you've never worn (including then), but it reminds you of that time in your life, it's OK to keep it. We understand.

- **Is it a collectible?** Sometimes our sentimental faves are better organized as personal "collections"—for example, a small group of items from our high school years or from the seventies and eighties. And as Garza says, it's OK to have collections (as long as we reorganize them properly).

2. **STEP TWO, DAY ONE:** The Easy Toss Out

- **Write it down.** As you go along, be sure to carry a legal pad and a pen (we love a good pen—it somehow spurs us on!) and write down everything you toss, donate, and may want to add in.

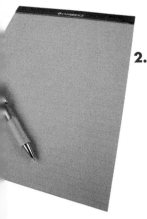

- **Toss.** That means *everything* above, with reservations as noted.

- **Bag it.** Do an instant toss that first full day. Your weapons of choice are a few simple garbage bags. Do not keep things to ponder unless they're truly nostalgic (a piece of clothing can be like a sentimental family photo) or you plan to donate them. And, yes, do donate, whether to Dress for Success, the Salvation Army, or your favorite local charity. *Put everything in big garbage bags—one to toss, one to donate—then do it.*

- **Let it sit.** *Elle* magazine's fashion news director Anne Slowey does leave the Maybes to ponder (and so do some of us) so it is an option—especially if pondering them becomes brain surgery. So if you're not sure about some items, do one of two things: Put them in another garbage bag labeled "Maybes" and leave it until the rest of your seven-day program period is over. Then promise yourself you'll act on it. You can also set aside a place in your home (some of us use the coat closet) for items you're not yet sure you can toss. But remember: Garza says you're better off tossing from the get go. And we agree.

> ## FFF WARDROBE WARNING
> Old handbags are an organizational no-no. As image consultant and closet-clutter expert Jesse Garza says, if you're keeping them from five years ago, don't. They will date your wardrobe instantly (and far more than other items). As for old bathing suits, they're a must-go, too. You deserve a fresh one every year.

3. **STEP THREE, DAY ONE:** The Try-Ons. As Garza notes, you must try clothes on as part of your day-one closet edit—no exceptions—otherwise you will block your fashion flow. Use your legal pad for any notations about what to try on based on the list below.

    - **Identify the regular situations in your life**—for example, a corpo-

rate job, dating, a few after-work cocktail parties, one black-tie affair a year, a few holiday parties, summer weekends at the beach; then ask yourself how often you go from day to evening, or are in too much of a rush to put together the right clothes.

- **Think outfits.** Then match the situation to the outfit—and make sure you plan your outfits head-to-toe. No matter what, have at least five to seven good, solid outfits that you feel really terrific in. If you try it on and it's borderline, cross it off your list.

- **Identify the add-ins.** Garza is adamant that this include replacing that drawer of old underwear, getting the new patterned hose you've been pondering and putting off, buying a new pair of one-of-a-kind earrings to replace the pair you left at the hairstylist and no one could find, or the pair of trendy sunglasses you lost at the gym. Anything that makes an outfit is a crucial add-in. And you must feel sexy. No exceptions, even if it's a pair of track pants for the gym—if you really need a cute top to go with it, list it.

THE SEEDING

And we continue, dear reader, with days two through four of your seven-day plan:

1. **GO SHOPPING—NOW!** Allow a few days for it, but not much more. *Season yourself*—get in the habit of filling in your wardrobe at the start of every season and, as Garza notes, as you discover what you need year-round. Consider this a start.

2. **BE A SUPPLY-SIDER.** Make sure you have enough of what you need—for instance, *Elle*'s expert Anne Slowey has *a drawer dedicated* to tank tops and in it she has an assortment that includes everything she needs for any occasion. She can dress in a hurry for anything—including a trip to Europe. You need to shop the same way.

REORGANIZING THE PERFECT CLOSET

Closet reorganization is so surprisingly controversial—there are as many ways to do it as there are experts out there—that we've decided, with much practice, to put together our own *FFF Tools and Rules for reorganizing the perfect closet:*

1. **LIKE ATTRACTS LIKE.** Sweaters go with sweaters, shirts with shirts, trousers with trousers, jackets with jackets. In your casual area, sweatshirts go with sweatshirts, shorts and track pants with track pants; put coats and other outerwear *together* in a coat closet.

2. **COLORS COORDINATE.** Within these categories, you want to put *like colors together*. Thus, if you're organizing your shirts, white can go on the left, a big group of colors in the middle, to make the closet "pop," as our celebrity stylist says, and then black and assorted neutrals on the right.

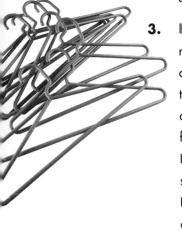

3. **HANG IT.** As Garza notes, you don't need to buy expensive hangers—plastic or wood will do. The key, as he notes, is to *be consistent*—make sure they're all one color (a fun color for plastic is fine), or if wood, the same shade. Include skirt and pants hangers of the same type for your items of that nature. Do not use clips (they dig into the fabric) or fold them over (they will crease). The one hanger exception involves your "current" sweaters—to prevent having to look at a stack of sweaters that are often the same color (we have ten or more black turtlenecks), hang

anything you wear now on a padded hanger—and make sure that the shoulders are squared with the hanger's tips to prevent bulges and creases; sweaters that are not current should be stacked on a shelf. Ditto for T-shirts: Put the "active" ones—this means the good ones you wear for work and more—on padded hangers (in color order, as noted above); stack your workout ones on a shelf. Again, you'll be able to see what you want to wear clearly.

4. **STEAM IT.** As Aguiar emphasizes (and does himself, along with nearly all of our celebrity stylists), buy yourself as high-quality a steamer as you can and get in the habit of giving your clothes a *quick once-over* any time you need to.

5. **PULL THE PLASTIC.** Remove any plastic from your clothes—it will turn colors like white yellow and otherwise ruin the fabric.

6. **LINE THE DRAWERS.** Garza prefers lavender paper that both wards off moths and smells and looks pretty.

7. **SACHET AWAY.** If you prefer this method, we won't stop you.

8. **PROVIDE FOR YOUR PANTS.** In addition to the good trousers on pants hangers that fold over, Anne Slowey suggests designating a jeans drawer (if you own a lot of them) and folding them in there. Keep your high-quality ones on *pants hangers*, too.

INSIDER SECRET

As celebrity stylist James Aguiar emphasizes (and does himself, along with nearly all of our celebrity stylists), buy yourself as high-quality a steamer as you can and get in the habit of giving your clothes a quick once-over any time you need to.

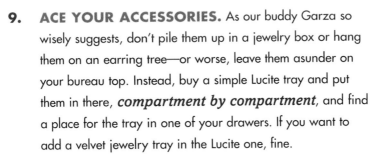

9. **ACE YOUR ACCESSORIES.** As our buddy Garza so wisely suggests, don't pile them up in a jewelry box or hang them on an earring tree—or worse, leave them asunder on your bureau top. Instead, buy a simple Lucite tray and put them in there, ***compartment by compartment***, and find a place for the tray in one of your drawers. If you want to add a velvet jewelry tray in the Lucite one, fine.

10. **KEEP THE GOWN AROUND.** Make sure you put your gowns and big-night-out dresses in ***long garment bags***—not the shorter ones you may receive from the store that can fold up the hem—and hang the bags in your closet.

11. **BAG YOUR COLLECTIONS.** Buy a canvas garment bag, says Garza, and put your sentimental faves (think newly named "collections") in it. Then put it in a far corner of your closet for safe keeping.

12. **RALLY THE RESORT.** Put every single thing you find that is for "resort" together. As Garza smartly points out, this ***grouping*** will help you save money on pricey replacements when you do decide to go away as many of us discover we don't need that last minute trip to Bergdorf's to pick up some new items; after all, they're all together now.

FFF WARDROBE WARNING

As closet-organizing pro Jesse Garza so wisely suggests, don't pile your accessories up in a jewelry box or hang them on an earring tree—or worse, leave them asunder on your bureau top. Instead, buy a simple Lucite tray and put them in there, compartment by compartment, and find a place for the tray in one of your drawers.

13. **BOX THE SHOES.** Our top choice via our celebrity stylists is to do what their A-list clients do and what's done backstage at the runway shows: *Put shoes in boxes* with Polaroids of the pair on the front. To do this, of course, you need to buy the camera and have the time and space. An insider secret: Remove your shoes from their boxes and place one shoe facing you and the mate facing away, then repeat. This way you'll be able to identify and grab your wares one-two-three while saving space. You can also buy a shoe bag—extra large—and hang it on the back of your closet door.

14. **MIND THE MIRROR.** If you don't have a three-way mirror—and we've encouraged you before—it's a *must-have* for the perfect closet.

15. **STEP ON IT.** If you put anything on a shelf you can't reach, make sure you don't need it very often—or buy a *step stool* that you can use easily. Make sure the stool is a nice one—not a plastic version that belongs in a basement.

16. **FILE THE HANDBAGS.** That's right. As Garza says, after you've edited out every single bag that isn't current, *line them up like files* on a shelf above your closet that you can see and reach.

17. **FILE THE HOSE.** In a drawer, do the same with your hose, in order from opaque to sheer; same for socks.

18. **WARDROBE THE WEEKEND.** If weekends away are a regular stint for you, put all your related *casual clothes together* and hang them neatly in the closet—preferably a different one from the one with your other clothes.

19. **TACKLE THE TRAVEL.** As we told you earlier, if you travel a lot, especially on tight schedules like we do, delegate a *travel drawer* and keep a separate set of makeup and toiletries, so you're always ready to go;

20. **BE A BEAUTY BEAST.** You've heard it but we can't say it enough—*after three months, toss it*. We mean mascara, old lipsticks, moisturizer bottles, blushers you never wear; if brushes haven't been washed in that time and you don't think you will, replace them now.

MAINTENANCE AND UPKEEP

Yep—it's a lot like dieting. Of the millions of people who lose weight, 98 percent gain it back. We're here to say you don't have to—as long as you do the above year-round. See it, toss it, donate it, replace it; always feel good in everything you have on display in your life.

Host HINT

Our host, Rebecca Budig, is astounded when she sees celebrity closets that are huge. How can they wear all those clothes? As both she and celebrity closet expert Garza will tell you, they can't. Even the most famous, they say, only need the outfits that are "active"—the rest can go.

the top ten

FFF EDITING YOUR CLOSET DOS AND DON'TS

DO

Salvage your sentimental favorites—They're like an old family photo.

Toss the ancient underwear—and socks; you deserve a regular refill.

Oversupply yourself—on things you adore and often wear. Think tanks and tees.

Use fold-over hangers for any pants and skirts—otherwise they will have maddening marks on them.

Buy a three-way mirror—it's a major must.

DON'T

Refuse to let go—as we know, the quick toss is boss.

Edit once a year—do it regularly, as you live your life.

Delay the donation!—it's a key part of editing your closet.

Stack the current clothes—you'll never find them in a hurry.

Forget to shop—NOW! Outfit add-ins are a must-do.

CHAPTER TEN

BECOME YOUR
OWN STYLIST

Dear Full Frontal Fashion:

If there's anything I really need to know about fashion, it's this:

How do I know what's "in"? I read the magazines, I watch the

TV shows, and I'm still not sure. Give me a hint, please!

TRENDLESS IN SEATTLE

Dear "Trendless," we know what you mean! Indeed, one of the biggest changes in fashion has been that the very cycle of fashion—how often the trends change—has sped up. It used to be that we'd buy something in 2005 and could count on it until 2009. Nowadays, as soon as something hits the runways (and the screens of our *Full Frontal Fashion* TV shows), there are companies out there copying the trends and, before you know it, they're in the stores for all of us to enjoy. That, of course, is the good news; the "bad," so to speak, is that we need to know so much more just to keep up. You're not alone in wondering whether that hobo bag from last season is still chic—or has it passed its peak? (Hint, hint: It's past its peak! And see our Accessories section on page 164!)

Now to the next big change: The advent of the stylist. There has been no bigger change in the history of fashion, perhaps, than the rise of this occupational group. Indeed, many members of our Full Frontal Fashion team of experts are stylists—for good reason. It is the stylist these days who puts the clothes together, on the runway, on the Broadway stage, or on the movie set. If you don't know how to mix it up like a pro, well, you're stuck with matched sets, which is so déclassé and passé (even when ladylike is a trend). Not to mention pricey.

Finally, if there's one stylist trick that works, it's this: As a beginner (and we don't mean this insultingly), your best bet is to create only one major fashion focal point (and this must always be a flattering one for your body type) per outfit—let's say, a wonderful jeweled belt, or a flattering hair color, or a handbag with a lot of texture to it. Then you can add additional foci as you move along in your styling life.

Here, we spill our FFF celebrity styling secrets on everything you need to know to put it all together—yes, *style*—like a pro.

FIT

Fit is it, folks. And we mean clothes that fit! Whether you speak to top celeb stylists, like own team pros, or a leading designer like Michael Kors, you will be told unequivocally that this is number-one on the expert advice circuit. As the *Wall Street Journal*'s senior special writer Teri Agins so wisely explains, clothes are designed to fit large numbers of people—not just you, dear reader.

So you must—we repeat *must*—begin with our two most important steps:

1. **GET THEE TO A TAILOR.** While some of our team pros say you have to go to a high-priced name-brand tailor for top-notch results, most of us have found just the opposite to be true: Our *neighborhood dry cleaners* have done wonderful work—for low rates and with overnight delivery, too. Not only that, we've discovered that we can barter with them, and save even more! But remember: Tailoring doesn't just mean pulling up a hem on your pants with a needle and some spare thread. Something as simple as a sleeve that is half an inch too long can make you appear inches shorter to the observer's eye; one that is too short can make your arms look stubby. Moreover, if the fit is off even a tiny degree, these tailoring "mistakes" will become the focal points of your outfit—so you don't even need to bother with the fashion foci you really want to catch the eye (think the jeweled accessory, the colorful top, the great big fun skirt à la Sarah Jessica Parker in *Sex and the City*).

2. **REDESIGN IN YOUR MIND.** Yes, we mean that! When we go shopping (and it took us time to learn this) we may see something we like—especially on sale—but maybe it's not the right size or even the perfect shape for us. If we adore it (one of us, for instance, recently fell for a beautiful light-blue satin blouse at a VIP designer sample sale), before we spill our currency at the cash register, we "redesign" it in our minds. In that instance, we knew

before we bought it that we needed to ask our trusty tailor or seamstress to take it in from the inner armhole to the base of the shirt to create an hour-glass; we knew that we needed to ask him or her to create more stylish three-quarter sleeves because they'd be more flattering than the original longer, more voluminous ones. Doing this before we decided to buy the shirt prevented this potentially gorgeous find from being a big balloon on the upper portion of our bodies. Our clever host, Rebecca Budig, redesigns in her mind all the time. "I learned from my experience with the soaps because a lot of things don't fit me," she says of her roles in leading soap operas. "I'm small and a lot of the time we have to reconstruct pieces. But in the end, I'm always very pleased because it's *the perfect fit*. So now I know I can have clothes I really like altered in different ways. I can really make them fit!"

3. **ACCENTUATE THE HOURGLASS.** Shape is the name of the styling game, whether you are Madonna or Gwen Stefani or Susan from Connecticut. Privately, our FFF stylists will tell you that with only rare excep-tions, tight is right. Basically, it is—even if you're heavier than you'd like to be—but please make sure you allow room to move so that, as we told you in the chapter on body types, you're not revealing "back fat," as our stylists pri-vately say, or "midriff meat." Keep this in mind when you shop, so you can try to save on tailoring expenses. Look for clothes that accentuate your hour-glass—a classic example is *a beautiful belted jacket* (safari for casual situations; jeweled for nighttime affairs; or add your own belt for an accessory-driven fit).

Host HINT

Our clever host, Rebecca Budig, has learned from her roles in leading soap operas—not to mention her hosting duties with us—that nothing is more important in the cloth-ing game than "redesigning in your mind." For example, if she falls in love with something that isn't a perfect fit—or perhaps doesn't even fit at all—she takes it to a tailor and has it reconstructed, sometimes from top to toe. "I know from TV that I can have clothes altered in different ways. I can really make them fit!"

PROPORTION

OK, you've passed step one. Now we move on to step two, which involves putting together the outfits themselves. Again, creating a nice, pretty hourglass shape is the key. The essentials for the start-up stylist are these:

1. **MAKE SURE YOU HAVE A BALANCING ACT GOING ON.** So, if you have a bigger item on top—say a wonderful white shirt with a slightly fuller sleeve and maybe a tad more room in the body itself (the designer Gianfranco Ferré is the style icon for this) or one of the latest bohemian, flow-y blouses or tunics—*make sure you pair it* with a pair of skinnier pants or you'll look heavier than you really are. Conversely, if you are wearing a pair of baggier pants, be sure to put a somewhat tighter-fitting top above it, and we suggest wearing a belt. You can also maintain an hourglass shape by pairing a nicely shaped jacket with a nicely shaped skirt—for instance, a fitted jacket with a pencil-style skirt. You can also go easy on yourself and just buy a shaped item—say, a wrap dress.

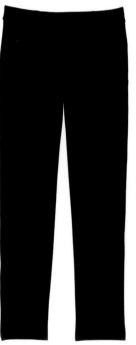

2. **SKIRT THE ISSUE.** If you're *balancing a skirt and a jacket* or coat, make sure that if the jacket is elongated, there's still a bit of skirt showing. If the jacket is shorter and fitted, make sure you maintain the hourglass with a skirt that is also shorter and fitted. The exception is if you're working with volume, which we'll tell you about soon.

PRINTS AND PATTERNS

Now we're truly graduating. Because mixing prints and patterns inappropriately can make you look big—and worse, like a style blunderer extraordinaire—we suggest this:

1. **REMEMBER: YOU'VE CREATED AN AUTOMATIC FOCAL POINT.** The minute you decide to wear *a print or pattern*—anywhere on your body—know that you have decided that this is your chosen focal point. We love floral skirts but when we wear them, we know that the observer's eye will go to our lower regions or our thigh area.

2. **CHOOSE YOUR FOCAL POINT WISELY.** Never is this more important than when you're moving into something as advanced as mixing pattern and print. As our style pro James Aguiar recommends, before selecting a piece of clothing with a lot going on, *decide what you want to accentuate*—and remember, as our pros stress, you can accentuate what others might consider to be your "flaws." The perfect example is the star Jennifer Lopez. She has a larger, well, you know, but when she dresses, she makes it a plus. If this were your choice, you might feel plenty comfy in a great pair of the latest patterned ladylike pedal-pushers.

3. **PLAY COLOR PICK-UP.** You want to choose at least one main color—or colors—in the pattern or print that you want to bring out in your other outfit pieces. For any starting stylist, we say, *one is enough!* So, if you do go with a great pair of patterned pedal-pushers, for instance, we suggest a solid top that picks up on one and only one color in the pattern, print, and/or design mix. And do make sure the color flatters your skin tone. As your styling know-how increases, go ahead and experiment with more than one color—witness our photos here, where our stylist James Aguiar has picked up on two shades—red and pink—from the floral skirt.

COLORS

As our FFF style team notes, you want to make sure of just two things:

1. **COLORS MUST BE FLATTERING.** The best way to make sure of this is to *hold the item up to your face* and judge whether it is a good match for your skin tone. Celebrity stylists like our own will hold up a bright white shirt, and if it makes you look brighter and more alive, it's the right white. If it makes you look sallow, it's not the right white. The same works for most colors: While a deeper or warmer tomato red livens up one person, a brighter, cooler red uplifts another. It takes practice—and for some, it's instinctive—but in the end, you'll know what shades were made for you. But remember: You do not need an expert for this—take your time and your color style will evolve.

2. **MATCH, DON'T CLASH.** As we on the Full Frontal Fashion style squad sit in our favorite cafés and stroll the streets of the world for our runway shows, we often see this blunder: the wearing of colors that create a palette, well, so pathetic that we want to turn away. If you're not sure whether the colors you're wearing match each other, ask a friend, a spouse, a boyfriend. And remember, your hair is a color, too, and so are your nails, and the lenses on those hot new lightweight sunglasses you love so much—so be sure to take the painting you're creating into account. *Be conscious of the colors* you wear most days—they're often your "instinctive" favorites—

INSIDER SECRET

As our celebrity style squad experts will tell you, the best way to determine if a color is flattering is to hold it up to your face to make sure it flatters your skin tone. If it does, you will look brighter and livelier; if it doesn't, well, you may just look as sallow as a lemon gone bad. To begin with, our style pro James Aguiar suggests, test-drive a bright white shirt and an ivory one.

before you decide to buy, say, those oval glasses with the dark frames or the fab new orange plastic ones with matching lenses. As we saw at a favorite celebrity eatery recently, without such styling awareness, you can be the clothing equivalent of a Jackson Pollock painting: Across from us sat a beautiful woman whose deep red hair clashed with the blue of her sexy V-neck, which clashed with the dark red nails she lifted to her glasses, which, with their light blue lenses clashed with both and the patterned scarf she had on.

3. **KEEP IT SIMPLE.** Indeed, we love starting the color game with a twinset that we pull apart—or that we buy in two shades to begin with. It's fun, chic, and clean.

TEXTURE

We on the Full Frontal Fashion style team are texture hounds. We just adore working with it, watching it on the runways, wearing it daily. You, dear reader, need to know just a few essentials to enjoy texturizing yourself as much as we do:

1. **TEXTURE IS EVERYWHERE.** It's easy enough to overlook, but anything that is not matte—in other words, flat—is basically textured. That means the studs on your belt, the basket weave of that new Chanel-style jacket, the cable knit of your favorite turtleneck sweater, the big pearl buttons on your otherwise man-tailored shirt. And we haven't even touched the *"surface,"* so to speak. Take, for example, some of the favorite items we have in our own styling "closet": a delicate, sheer evening shrug with feathers the length of chair legs, or quilted jackets and coats fashioned from an assortment of interesting fabrics. Recognize texture when you're getting dressed, or better yet, shopping for clothes, and you're on your way.

2. **TEXTURE-EYES.** Any time you texturize, you will capture the observer's eye. It is an instant fashion focal point. So we say, if you're about to buy a great white-leather belt with studs on it, be aware that the observer's eye will go to your waistline; if you also own a leather jacket with studs on the sleeves and you plan to wear it with the belt, the observer's eye will go to both. So, ask yourself, again, *"What do I want to accentuate?* My shapely waist, perhaps?" and "Am I complicating the view by showing off two textures?"

3. **KEEP IT CLEAN.** We basically advised you of this key styling point above, but we say, in more detail, if you wear one texture—we fell in fashion love with a wonderful coat with a raffia feel to it—it's better that you put a simple Audrey Hepburn–style sheath underneath it instead of anything with a pattern or texture. It creates a beautiful canvas for your showier item; moreover, the look itself is chic, stylish, and, best of all, clean and streamlined, which we adore. Finally, an FFF Wardrobe Warning:

Be sure to *limit yourself to one texture* when it comes to accessories, too—unless you work at a fashion mag. For most of us, though, if our shoes have texture to them—such as nubby fabric, a bow, or a pierced strap—we say, wear it solo and always know that's where our eyes will go.

FFF WARDROBE WARNING

Be sure to limit yourself to one texture when it comes to accessories, too—unless you work as an editor or stylist for a fashion mag. For most of us, though, if our fave shoes have texture to them—nubby fabric, a bow, jewels and/or two tones—we say, wear them solo and always know that's where everyone's eyes will go.

VOLUME

This isn't far removed from proportion, but sometimes the wonderful hourglass we talked about becomes exaggerated—especially if you've watched enough TV shows like *Sex and the City*. The rule here are simple:

1. **EXERCISE VOLUME CONTROL.** If the skirt is a ballet style that is almost as big as you are, make sure the top is tight and fitted. Also, *you may not want to do this too often*—it's fun, but doesn't look good on everyone.

2. **EXTEND YOUR VOLUME-KNOW HOW.** Do this through-out your wardrobe. If you're wearing fuller pants, for instance, look for a sleek, fitted blouse. And remember: If you're not the full-pants type (see Chapter 7) stick to narrower ones.

LAYERING

Nothing gets our style pros going like the opportunity to create layers—indeed they do it so instinctively that when we ask them to explain it for you, dear reader, they barely can. But we know what to tell you!

1. **DON'T BE A MAG HAG.** While you may see a print shirt under a pinstriped vest under yet another jacket with the whole shebang under a coat and, added to that, a removable fur collar, we want you to know that many mags—and ads, for that matter—are trying to sell you something, so they've layered as many items into the mix as they can so you can see them and ultimately decide what to buy. In real life, off the runways (dear reader, know that the runways are sales tools, too!) we say, layer *no more than three items*—for instance, a T-shirt under a long sleeve henley-style tee, under a jacket; or a long-sleeve shirt and a couple of tanks discreetly layered with one essentially serving as a vest; or, as we saw on one stylish movie star with a very normal body, a white leotard under a lacey white shirt under a great featherweight striped jacket with rolled up sleeves to show off her cuffs.

2. **BE COLOR CONSISTENT.** If you're layering neutrals (black, white, camel), stay with neutrals; if you're layering brights, stay with brights, or mix them with neutrals; if you're going for a full court press and layering prints and patterns, we say, again, *be careful*—that plaid top under that pinstriped vest under that floral jacket does make a great celebrity ad (we loved it when we saw it!) but it's a real life no-go (unless your Fashion Personality is Eccentric or you've just been hired to style a fashion shoot).

DAY FOR EVENING

The late, great designer Bill Blass is the style icon here and we love everything he put on the map—nothing more so than the simple notion of a casual or sporty item with an item that is dressier (the word he would have used is "sportswear" and it's the fashion category that put American fashion on the map as compared to its more serious, and perhaps even trendier, European counterparts). The result will take you from day to night and back again, and then some. Here is the insider style trick:

1. **OUTFIT IS OUTCOME.** This is all about planning ahead—knowing what the situations are in your life that you need to dress for, and how you're going to do it. If you need clothes that go to the office—or to a cocktail party or wedding brunch or first date or big date night out—and you don't want to spend money on more than one outfit, you want to go Day for Evening. One pick we love from our stylist on tap, James Aguiar, is a wonderful staple like a fitted lace blouse (the dressier piece) worn with a tweed skirt (the more casual one). You can also go with another fave of ours—a lightweight evening skirt (think a wonderful chiffon skirt like the one in our Travel chapter) with a more casual sleeveless cashmere turtleneck that you can also pair with jeans (as you can with the great lace top, too).

ACCESSOR-EYES

Yes indeed, updating with accessories is our fave. Next to that is knowing that when it comes to catching the observer's eye—and moving it to our favorite spots, nothing works better—or is easier. Here are our top two tips:

1. **MAKE A STATEMENT.** As we told you in the RSVP chapter, under the brilliant aegis of our accessories style pro, Irenka Jakubiak of *Accessories*

magazine, you want to make *one accessories statement per outfit*. The best way to do that is to buy yourself statement pieces and wear them regularly. And remember this once again: You don't have to spend an arm and a leg to look chic. Our picks and Jakubiak's, too: a great-looking watch that says you're fine with the promotion and you're fine without. Think one with diamonds (or fab fakes) instead of something more common, demure, and ladylike. Another pick: a great cocktail ring or a great big pair of earrings. On the latter, though, be forewarned: treat any colored stones as a color. If you're wearing a floral skirt with a blue in it that looks good on you, you may want to pick it up by buying a big pair of chandeliers with bluish stones (and keep the rest of the jewelry quiet). You can also create a great look with a statement piece that's worn against a stark canvas. Just the other day we saw raven-haired Tamara Edison, a translator, looking beautifully stylish in black jeans, a black quilted jacket, her already deep-dark hair (worn casually in a messy updo) and nothing more than an oversized pair of decorative gold hoops. It brought our eye to her best accessory—her smile. You can also tailor your statement pieces to your neckline (please see Chapter 3), and that neckline doesn't have to be on an evening gown—the same rules apply.

2.   **HAIR IS THERE.** Our pros have said it over and over again—don't forget that your *hair catches the observer's eye* like any other part of your wardrobe. Its color *is* a color; if it's up with hair ornaments, that is statement enough and you don't need much or any jewelry or other wardrobe goings-on, other than a monochromatic canvas; if it's going even subtly gray and you rinse that out, not only will you drop years and look hipper, but the eye will be more likely to go places other than to register the fact that you need to cover your gray. Moreover, you can do it at home for very little money. And, as Agins said so strongly in our body types chapter, if you can't keep your streaks perfectly streaked, don't go there to begin with.

KNOWING WHAT'S IN

Dear "Trendless," our savvy FFF e-mailer, you hit the style nail on its head as to the real insider know-how so we save your insightful query for next to last. And we say, finally, to remember two things:

1. **START "OUT."** By this we mean it's a lot easier to know what's "out" than what's "in." All we need to do is take a lead from Jesse Garza, the world-class image consultant who told us how to *edit our cluttered closets*. If you have clothes that you no longer wear, be brutal and edit them out. And let us say from experience that if you're not wearing it, it isn't in— at least for you. If you're female (and we assume most of our readers are) this essential "out" edit is second to breathing, once you become conscious of it. We promise you.

2. **READ THE MAGS, LOOK AT THE ADS, AND WATCH TV SHOWS LIKE OURS.** You'll get the trend alerts. But do not go lemming-like into that fashion good night.

3. **UPDATE WITH ACCESSORIES.** The easiest way to update your wardrobe is with accessories (the converse is true, too—the easiest way to look out of style is with last season's accessories). So *seasonalize* the way our about-to-be married Date chapter pal Susan Zelnick does so well: At the start of each season, take the measure of your wardrobe, schedule a shopping trip, and add a new bag and a new shoe. If the round toe is now "in," toss the pointy ones; if last year's tote now feels remote, say good-buy to an "in" clutch; if the clutch feels like dust, well, then go out and get the latest baguette. Another great way to work with accessories is to buy a new pair of trendy sunglasses—be they aviators, big Jackie O.'s or cat eyes. And again, ice the price pressure. One of us found a great trendy pair (originally about three hundred dollars) online for under twenty-five.

4. **TREND-ICIZE.** We say, *one trend* is enough. More than that and you may look like a bad abstract painting. Example: We adore—repeat adore—a Mandarin-style jacket. And that one trendy item is all you need. Just wear it with a pair of sleek trousers (we love a great pair of dark jeans—the really high quality ones author and style expert Lloyd Boston says we must have in the Casual chapter)—or a basic skirt. Do note, dear reader and e-mailer, that this "Mao" jacket is "in" as we write this chapter but you can go with any of the current season's "trendy" toppers. Do know, however, that apart from its current trendiness, we also love an Asian-style jacket because it's enough of a stylish classic that we can recycle it next time around—simply wear it as if it were one of a kind and also put it on day, night, and in-between. It's just perfect.

THE CONFIDENCE TO GO

We started there and we'll end there. Nothing is more important to us and to the observer's eye than your love of yourself—at least in terms of what we can do via the wardrobe. And as James Aguiar, our celeb stylist, says, on this last note:

"Feel good in what you wear. If you don't feel good about yourself in it, do not wear it."

Period. End of sentence. End of book.

FFF BECOME YOUR OWN STYLIST
DOS AND DON'TS

DO

Decide what you want to accentuate —and it doesn't have to be the body part everyone else says you should.

Wear only one big trend—otherwise you'll look like a Christmas tree in summer.

Accessor-eyes with statement pieces—we love a rich-looking watch, big stylish earrings, a chic cocktail ring.

Pick your prints and patterns— carefully. Start with one and move on from there.

Take care with your hair—it's as much of a wardrobe element and eye-catcher as anything else you put on.

DON'T

Pump up the volume—unless you know how to exercise volume control.

Forget that style is a balancing act— big on top means small on bottom, and that's just for starters.

Wear clashing colors—start by knowing what looks good with your skin tone; then choose one or two shades that work well together.

Wear last year's handbag—nothing says "in" like a new one.

Leave home without the confidence to go—if you're a sad sack, it may just be the sack you're wearing.

CREDITS

Special thanks to the following designers and retailers whose clothing, accessories, and beauty products were used in this book:

A. Cheng

ABS by Allen Schwartz

AG Jeans by Adriano
  Goldschmied

Akris

Alberta Ferretti

Alex and Ani Jewelry

Anne Klein Watches

Ann Taylor Loft

apt. 5 cosmetics

Banana Republic

Barneys New York

BCBG MAXAZRIA

Ben Sherman USA

Berettoti

Bergdorf Goodman

Betsey Johnson

Bruno Cucinelli

Burberry

Buzz by Jane Fox

Calvin Klein Collection

Casting

Cejon Scarves

Celine

Century 21 Department
  Stores

Chetta B

Chloé

Chocolate Skate Warehouse

Christian Dior

Ciarla by Jessica Ciarla

CK by Calvin Klein

Club Monaco

Coach

Colgate

D&G by Dolce & Gabbana

Dana Buchman

Diane von Furstenberg

Diesel USA

DKNY Donna Karan New
  York

Catherine Malandrino

DKNY Watches

dollhouse New York

Echo Scarves

Eddie Rodriguez

Ellen Tracy

Elie Tahari

Emilio Pucci

Evisu

Express

French Connection

Felina

Fossil

Frank & Kahn Accessories

Giorgio Armani Le Collezioni

Guess?

H by Tommy Hilfiger

H&M by Hennes and Mauritz

Hanes

Heavy Rotation

ID at the Hat Shoppe

J.Crew

JLo by Jennifer Lopez

James Perse

JCPenney

Jewelry.com

Joe's Jeans

John Galliano

Jou Jou

Jurlique

Karl Lagerfeld for H&M

kate spade

Kenneth Cole

L'Occitane en Provence

Lacoste

Lambertson Truex

Linda Youngs Hawaiiana

Lipo in a Box

Loehmann's

Lord & Taylor

Macy's

Magu

Marc Jacobs

Marina Rinaldi

Mexx

Miss Trish of Capri

Moschino

Moschino Cheap & Chic

Nancy Nancy

nanette lepore

Nicole Miller

Nine West Handbags

Nordstrom

Olive and Bette's Boutique

Only Hearts

Oscar de la Renta

Philosophy di Alberta Ferretti

Piazza Sempione

Pleats Please by Issey Miyake

Polo Jeans Co. Ralph Lauren

Postcard

Pure Accessories

Ralph by Ralph Lauren

Ralph Lauren

rebecca taylor

Revlon

Ricky's NYC

Robert Best

Saks Fifth Avenue

Salvatore Ferragamo

Sama Eyewear

Samsonite

Sequin

Seven for All Mankind

Shanghai Tang

shin choi

Singer Sewing Machines

Skinceuticals

Spanx by Sara Blakely

Stacey Hasse

Stuart Weitzman

Ted Baker London

The Container Store

theory

Tiara Misu

Tommy Hilfiger

Tse Cashmere

Tse Say

Unis

Victoria's Secret

What Goes Around Comes Around Vintage

Y & Kei

Yochi Design

Zara

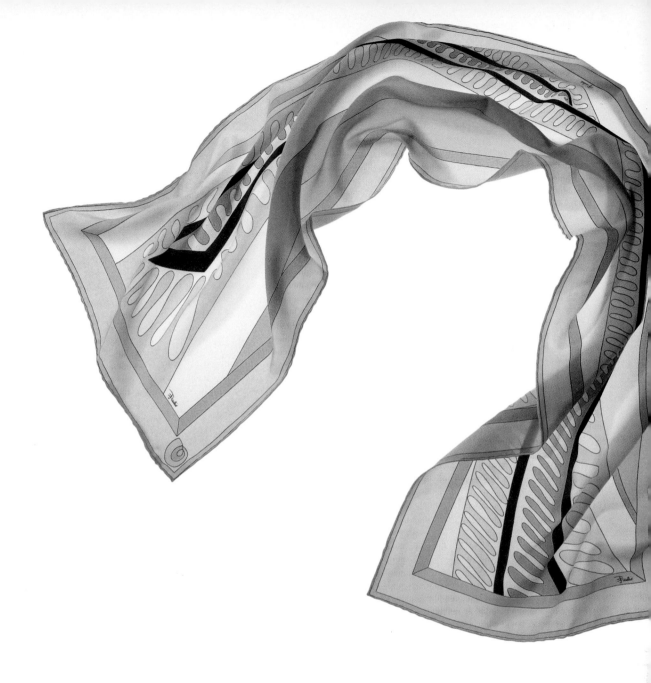